Vanishing Landmarks of Georgia

"Something about a gristmill makes time stand still."

Andrew Sparks
Atlanta Journal
May 5, 1957

Vanishing Landmarks of Georgia

Gristmills & Covered Bridges

TEXT & PHOTOGRAPHY BY JOSEPH KOVARIK

JOHN F. BLAIR, PUBLISHER · WINSTON-SALEM, NC

JOHN F. BLAIR,
P U B L I S H E R

1406 Plaza Drive
Winston-Salem, North Carolina 27103
www.blairpub.com

PRINTED AND BOUND IN INDIA BY IMPRINT PRESS

Library of Congress Cataloging-in-Publication Data

Names: Kovarik, Joseph, 1946-
Title: Vanishing landmarks of Georgia : gristmills & covered bridges / by
    Joseph Kovarik.
Description: Winston-Salem, North Carolina : John F. Blair, Publisher, 2016.
    | Includes index.
Identifiers: LCCN 2016021960 (print) | LCCN 2016025607 (ebook) | ISBN
    9780895876706 (pbk. : alk. paper) | ISBN 9780895876713 (ebook) | ISBN
    9780895876713
Subjects: LCSH: Georgia—Tours. | Historic sites—Georgia—Guidebooks. |
    Automobile travel—Georgia—Guidebooks. | Gristmills—Georgia—Guidebooks.
    | Covered bridges—Georgia—Guidebooks.
Classification: LCC F284.3 .K68 2016 (print) | LCC F284.3 (ebook) | DDC
    917.58/04—dc23
LC record available at https://lccn.loc.gov/2016021960

10 9 8 7 6 5 4 3 2 1

Cover photo : Berry College Mill; photo on page viii: Bay's Bridge
Cover design by Anna Sutton

This book is dedicated to Denise Mowder and the memory of Scott Foremny. On the worst day of her life, Denise lost her son Scott. She made the difficult decision to donate his organs, thus saving several lives, including mine.

If you are an organ donor, please inform your family. If you are not an organ donor, please consider doing so. It saves lives.

Lefler Mill

Table of Contents

Acknowledgments

I could not have written this book without the assistance and cooperation of many people. Mill owners were gracious enough to welcome me to their properties and allow me to roam around their grounds while photographing the mills. They also took time to let me interview them regarding their property.

Many times, members of county historical societies provided me with copies of land records and old newspaper clippings. Special thanks to: Judy Alderman, Penny Cliff, Rena Cobb, James Cunningham, Calvin Dalton, Marie Drake, Shanna English, Missy Garner, Gene Griffith, Lawson Hearon, Angie Hix, Mark Jackson, Michael Johnson, Elizabeth Jones, Christopher Loos, Jimmy Madden, Tommy Martin, Forbes Matthews, David McDonald, Herman Miller, Ann Moore, Keith Norris, Russ Page, Peggy Payne, Scarlett Sears, Keith and Kristine Stowers, and Joe Vandegriff.

Thank you also to Barry Brown and Janet Cochran of the Georgia Department of Economic Development, who provided advice and support.

Patrick Allen of University of Georgia Press provided early advice and was one of the first to recognize the merits of the book.

My wife Shari Kovarik, my sister Susan Kovarik, and Mike Ciletti provided much of the initial editing and encouragement to complete this project.

I would be remiss if I did not thank Carolyn Sakowski of John F. Blair, Publisher. Her final editing, proofing, and fact checking were an invaluable contribution to the book. Her attention to detail and thorough reviews made this a better book.

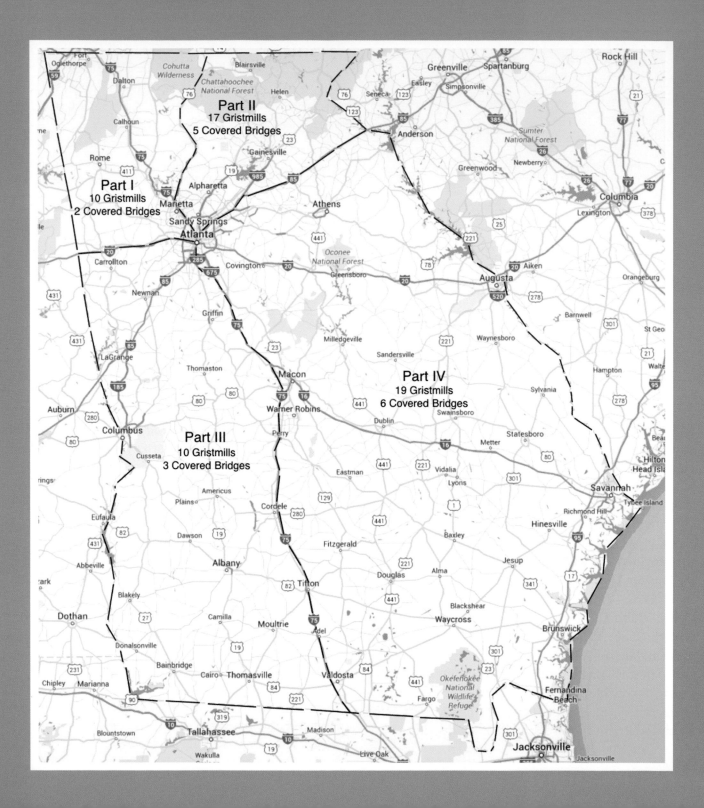

Introduction

Universally, people throughout the United States are fascinated by old mills and covered bridges. These structures are often the focal points of books, movies, and artwork. Usually located in bucolic settings, these mills and bridges represent a time when craftsmen built structures to last.

Georgia's history stretches back to colonial times. During that time, gristmills and covered bridges played important roles in developing the state's economy. The covered bridges were key links within Georgia's transportation system. The gristmills were the precursors of Georgia's industrialization. Harnessing the water power of the streams eventually led to the growth of textile and electrical industries on the major rivers of the state.

This book attempts to document a rapidly disappearing past by providing a guide to over 70 of these structures still standing in Georgia at the time this book was written.

Gristmills

In the early days of Georgia settlement, there were no gristmills. The early settlers of Georgia were isolated, so cornmeal production was done individually with a one-handed wooden pestle and log mortar.

At first, settlers increased production by taking a one-handed pestle and mortar and expanding it to use two stones about two feet in diameter. Originally a two-man device, it was easily adapted so it could be driven by animals. In the 1730s, this new development, which was called a horse mill, was first built in Savannah. The mill quickly fell into disrepair. Because Savannah was an ocean port, there was no need to repair the mill because it was easier to import flour and cornmeal.

The first water-powered mill was built on the Ebenezer River circa 1740. In 1935, the Ebenezer River mill, which used a wooden undershot wheel, was reportedly still in operation. Unfortunately, it is no longer standing.

Settlers gradually began to migrate upriver and settle in the creek valleys. As the population increased, many communities supported a local mill, which allowed easy transport of the grain from the fields to the mill. Because bread was an important part of the farmers' diet, the mill became integral to the region's well-being. As migration moved west and north, the number of mills increased. The roads were poor, so the mills were relatively small and served those who lived within roughly a ten-mile radius.

But the local mill was more than a place to convert grain to cornmeal or flour. Mills also served as community gathering places. At harvest time, the entire family transported its grain crop to the mill site. For the men, it was a business trip to sell the harvest and exchange information on crop seed and farm techniques. For the women, it was an opportunity to leave the normal drudgery of nineteenth-century homemaking. Here, they could catch up on community news and discuss the latest changes in the homemakers' routines with other women. For the children, it was a rare opportunity to meet old friends they hadn't seen in months and to make new friends.

Water powered most gristmills, though wind or livestock powered some. The fall of the water or the "head" determined a mill's power. In Georgia, mills were most prevalent along the fall line, the geological break between the piedmont and coastal plain portions of the state. Here, the head increased over a short distance as rivers and streams crossing the fall line provided a convenient source of power. Placement of mills in the piedmont or Cumberland Plateau was dependent on the topography. Mills were placed below shoals or waterfalls to obtain the necessary head. In areas where the topography did not provide sufficient head, dams were built to provide sufficient fall to power the mill.

A mill site consisted of the water source, a means of conveying the water to the mill (a head race), the wheel pit, a waterwheel, a system of shafts, gears, and pulleys to drive the mill, and a means of returning the water to the stream (a tailrace).

There were a variety of waterwheels. The most common was the overshot wheel, which used paddles or buckets to catch the water as it poured over the wheel. The wheel turned in the same direction as the water flow. The overshot wheel was fairly easy to construct and provided a large amount of power. The drawback was that it was difficult to regulate the flow. As water exited the buckets at mid-wheel height, the backsplash created problems, affecting the miller's ability to maintain a wheel's RPM.

Another frequently used type of wheel was the breastshot wheel. The water entered at the mid-point of the side of the wheel, turning in the opposite direction of the water flow. These wheels produced minimal backsplash. Most gristmills in early Georgia used either the overshot or breastshot wheel.

A third type of wheel was the undershot wheel, driven primarily by the current of the river. The undershot wheel was easier to construct but produced less power. It was used primarily on smaller farms or plantations.

A modification of the undershot wheel was the tub wheel. It was essentially the undershot wheel turned on its side and placed within a circular box. This wheel often allowed for the direct drive of the millstones without the use of gears and pulleys.

The water wheel was limited in the amount of power that it could develop efficiently. In the mid-nineteenth century as the mills got larger and required more power, the turbine was developed. The main difference between the water wheel and the turbine was the swirl component added to the normal water flow. This additional motion component allowed the turbine to be smaller, even though it produced as much or more power than the water wheel. Additionally, the miller could adjust the turbine's speed by simply adjusting the inlet gate.

The power generated by the water carried by overshot, undershot, and breastshot wheels turned a system of gears, pulleys, and belts. Because the water flow itself was difficult to control, the gears, pulleys, and belts allowed the miller to regulate the power to the mill drive. The gears, pulleys, and belts connected to a vertical shaft running through two millstones. The lower stone was fixed while the upper stone rotated. Grain was poured into an opening in the upper stone and was ground between the stones. The stones had grooves cut into them to allow the ground grain to eventually exit for further processing.

It's impossible to know exactly how many gristmills there were in Georgia. During the Civil War, General William Sherman ordered his Union troops to destroy all factories in his famous "March to the Sea" from Chattanooga to Savannah. Although Sherman specifically exempted the local gristmills, still many were destroyed because Southern patriots hid parts of machinery or they disabled the mill to keep them from being used by Sherman's troops.

In 1876, the Georgia Department of Agriculture's records show there were 1,262 water-powered mills in the state. The 1900 census shows 1,123 gristmills.

The number of water-powered gristmills began to decline when the easy availability of steam and gas engines replaced the water wheel. As population and grain production increased, the mills switched to a process where grain was crushed between steel hammers or rollers rather than between two large stones. Because this was a more efficient process, the mills grew larger, economically squeezing out the small local gristmill.

Today, very few mills are left standing. In their

Overshot water wheel

Water Flow

Flume

Wheel Rotation

Tail race

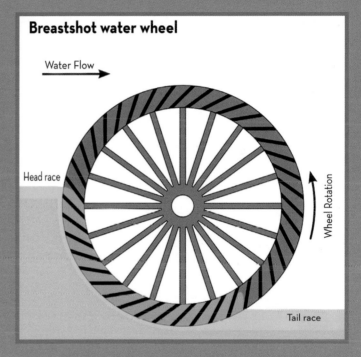

Breastshot water wheel

Water Flow

Head race

Wheel Rotation

Tail race

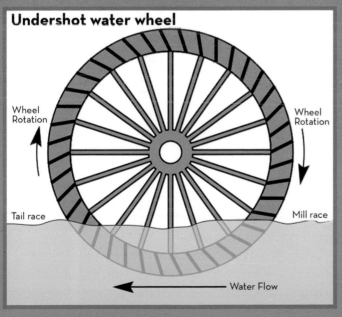

Undershot water wheel

Wheel Rotation

Wheel Rotation

Tail race

Mill race

Water Flow

Georgia mill database, Society for the Preservation Of Old Mills (SPOOM) lists approximately 300 mills. This list includes textile mills, cotton gins, and sites that are either only ruins or only the historical location of a vanished mill.

This book identifies 56 mills still standing that would be of interest to the general public. Some mills are operational; some may be in a deteriorating state. Most can be visited or seen from the road. There are some mills that require prior permission to visit. I have noted those instances in their description. If the reader is interested in identifying additional mill locations, consult the SPOOM website at http://www.spoom.org.

Covered Bridges

The first covered bridges in the United States were built around the beginning of the nineteenth century. The early bridges were essentially logs laid across a stream or river. Eventually, this method of water crossing evolved into longer spans using trusses, arches, and stringers. The earliest bridges were made of wood and exposed to the elements. The exposure to wind and water accelerated deterioration of the wooden elements used in bridge construction. To protect the wood from the elements and prolong the life of the bridge, builders began to cover the bridges. Covering the bridge increased its stability. The added weight also made the bridge less susceptible to floods.

In Georgia, most of the covered bridges are of the Town's Lattice Truss design, which consists of a large number of small and closely spaced diagonal elements that form a lattice often joined by wooden pegs. There are no vertical elements on this type of bridge. The diagonal elements take both compression and tension load. This design allows a long span of 50 to 220 feet.

Another covered bridge design is the King Post. This is the simplest of the covered bridge structures. It consists of a bottom chord or span with two diagonal members meeting at the center vertical post. It is a simple construction, but it is limited to a short span length of 20-60 feet.

A third type of construction is the Queen Post. This is a lengthened version of the King Post except it uses two vertical posts connected by a horizontal top member. This construction is still simple but allows for a longer span of 20-80 feet.

Historically, there were covered bridges throughout Georgia but over time they were replaced with concrete and steel bridges, eliminating the need to cover them.

According to www.dalejtravis.com., if you include decorative, modern, and commercial development, there are over 80 covered bridges in Georgia. For the purposes of this book, I've included only those bridges listed by the Georgia Department of Transportation, except for one that is located in a state park.

How to Use the Book

Since the gristmills and bridges in this book are scattered throughout the state, for convenience, the state is divided into four sections with Atlanta as the hub. See the accompanying map on page x:

Part I—The Northwest section is bordered by I-75/I-575/US 76 on the east and I-20 on the south. It has ten gristmills and two covered bridges.

Part II—The Northeast section is bordered by I-75/I-575/US 76 on the west and I-85 on the south. It has seventeen gristmills and five covered bridges.

Part III—The Southwest section is bordered on the north by I-20 and I-75 on the east. It has ten gristmills and three covered bridges.

Part IV—The Southeast section is bordered on the west by I-75 and on the north by I-85. It has nineteen gristmills and six covered bridges.

To aid those who wish to visit the mill or bridge sites,

the locations are grouped together for travel in a general direction from west to east. These groupings should allow you to visit as many sites as possible on a single tour.

In each mill site's listing, you'll find how the mill is powered and the body of water it uses. Each covered bridge listing includes the type of construction design and the body of water it crosses. All have listings for the street address, a telephone number, a website address, and hours are provided if applicable.

Each profile gives driving directions, beginning from a nearby town that is easy to find on a map. For each site, the Georgia Department of Economic Development Tourism's region is included. This will allow the reader to use Georgia's official Tourism and Travel Site, www.exploregeorgia.org to plan for other activities.

There is a map for each of the four regions that notes the locations of the sites in that region. These regional maps will help the reader get a perspective of the site's location relative to a major road or city.

For each site there are GPS coordinates. The coordinates are in degrees, minutes, and seconds (xx° yy' zz"). Sites converting Decimal degree (xx.xxxx°), GPS (xx yy.yy) or UTM are readily available online. The GPS location is of the mill or bridge or in some cases the entrance to the park in which the site is located. Use caution when using a GPS since roads used in the mapping system may not be open or passable and your GPS navigator may not find a satellite signal in some areas.

There is also a brief description and history of the mill or bridge. Occasionally, other nearby sites of interest are included.

Not all the sites are open to the public, but unless otherwise noted, they are visible from a public road or park. Please respect the property owners of these sites and do not trespass on private property.

In researching the history of each site, I often found conflicting information. I have tried to include the information provided by the most reliable source. Often-times, I relied on personal interviews with the current owners for background.

I personally visited and photographed each of the sites. All the photographs were taken from a public location or were taken on the property with the owner's permission.

This last paragraph of a 1953 *Georgia Review* article talks about the disappearance of Georgia's gristmills:

> The old, dilapidated grist mill with its moss-covered water wheel has earned a place in our history that goes beyond fond memories of childhood. As the oldest continuously conducted industry known to mankind and the first to be completely mechanized, it has played an essential role in our economy. Let us hope that a few of the old mills will be preserved to remind us that life was not always a matter of turning dials and pushing buttons.

A similar sentiment about preservation can be applied to Georgia's covered bridges. When the article was written, it recognized that these structures needed to be preserved. Yet in the intervening time, the 600 gristmills that stood in 1953 have diminished to less than 75 and only 12 are operational.

The mills and bridges provide a glimpse into a past that is rapidly disappearing. We drive through on the freeways at 70 MPH barely seeing what Georgia has to offer as we race to our destination. Taking the time to find these vanishing landmarks forces us to slow down, drive the back roads, and absorb the variety, history, and culture of Georgia's bygone days. I've enjoyed photographing these historical locations and hope that you will take the slow road and enjoy these icons of the past. If you know of a mill or bridge not listed here, I would appreciate if you would contact me via email at josephpkovarik@hotmail.com with the description and location for future editions.

Gresham's Mill

PART I
The Northwest

The Northwest section has two distinct geological regions—the Appalachian plateau in the very northwest corner and the series of valleys and ridges that transition from the plateau. The plateau region reaches a height of 2,400 feet at Lookout Mountain; the series of ridges and valleys form a line from the Tennessee border southwest towards Cedartown. This geology creates many streams and rivers that have enough fall to allow the building of water-powered gristmills. This section of the book includes ten gristmills and two covered bridges.

1 Lee and Gordon's Mills
2 Prater's Mill
3 Dennis Mill
4 Berry College Mill
5 Old Brick Mill in Lindale aka
   Hoss Mill aka Barnett's Mill
   aka Jones's Mill
6 Euharlee Covered Bridge
7 Gresham's Mill aka Sixes Mill
8 The Old Mill aka Benedicts
   Mill
9 Pine Mountain Gold Mine Mill
10 Concord Covered Bridge &
   Ruff's Mill
11 Lefler Mill aka Pine Run Mill
   aka Life University
   Gristmill

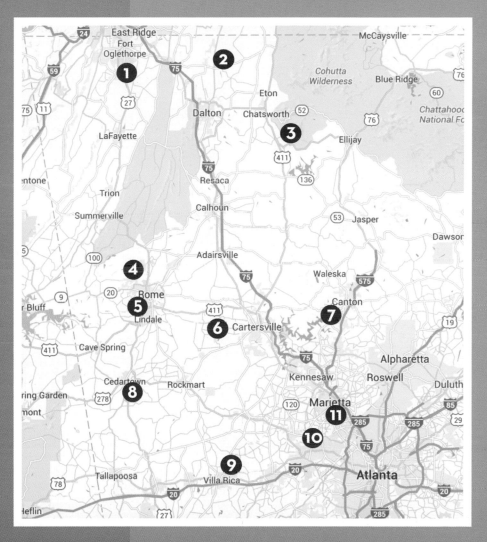

A cannon memorializes the occupation by both Confederate and Union armies during the Chickamauga campaign in 1863. The mill lies just a few miles south of the Chickamauga and Chattanooga National Military Park.

1 Lee and Gordon's Mills

Powered by: Turbine

Water body: West Chickamauga Creek

71 Red Belt Road, Chickamauga 30707

706-375-6801

leeandgordonsmills.com

Hours: Tues.-Sat. 9 AM-5 PM

N34 53 01.2 W85 16 00.7

Tourism Region: Historic High Country

Raceway for Lee and Gordon's Mills

DRIVING DIRECTIONS

Driving on I-75 about 10 miles from the Tennessee border, take Exit 350. Proceed west 6.5 miles. Take the exit for US 27 South (Frank M. Gleason Parkway). Go to the third traffic signal (approximately 5.5 miles). At that signal, turn left. Proceed until you reach a stop sign. At the stop sign, turn right (*Note:* the turn is almost 180 degrees). Travel to the second gate. Turn left and go through the gate. The mill is immediately in front of you.

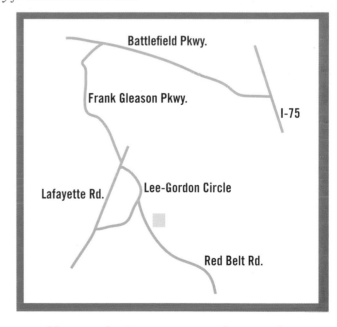

HISTORY

The Gordon brothers moved to Crawfish Springs (later renamed Chickamauga) in 1836. James Gordon built the original mill with an attached storeroom and general store. After the original mill burned down, the present building was built in 1867. Over the years, the mill changed hands several times. Bill and Charley Wallace operated the mill until they retired and decided to shut down the mill in 1967. It sat idle until 1995 when it was sold to Frank Pierce. He spent the next six years restoring the mill, dam, and machinery to its original condition. It reopened in 2001. Today the mill still grinds corn, just as it did in 1836.

Prater's Mill

2 Prater's Mill

Powered by: Turbine
Water body: Coahulla Creek
5845 GA 2, Dalton 30721
706-694-6455
www.pratersmill.org
Hours: Open to the public during daylight hours.
N34 53 44 W84 55 11.6
Tourism Region: Historic High Country

Prater's Mill

DRIVING DIRECTIONS

Drive northeast from Dalton on I-75. Exit at GA 201 (Exit 341). Travel north 4.5 miles to GA 2. Turn right and continue 2.6 miles to Prater's Mill.

HISTORY

In 1855, Benjamin Franklin Prater built Prater's Mill on Coahulla Creek. It was originally just a grain mill but as it became more popular, a cotton gin, sawmill, wool carder, syrup mill, general store, and blacksmith shop were added. The mill was not destroyed during the Civil War.

The Prater family operated it until the 1950s. A volunteer foundation took over the mill and began restoration preservation efforts in 1971. Unfortunately, in 1995, arsonists set the mill on fire, causing significant damage to the interior and the roof. The foundation is currently soliciting donations to repair the mill. Today the mill holds an arts-and-crafts fair twice a year. The site is popular for fishing, cookouts, and family reunions.

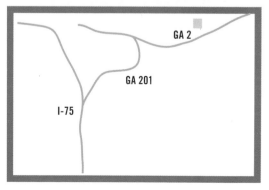

Dennis Mill

3 Dennis Mill

Powered by: Overshot wheel

Water body: Rock Creek

634 Dennis Mill Road, Chatsworth 30705

678-697-6985

Facebook: Dennis-Mill-Cabin

N34 42 06.8 W84 42 31.6

Tourism Region: Historic High Country

Dennis Mill

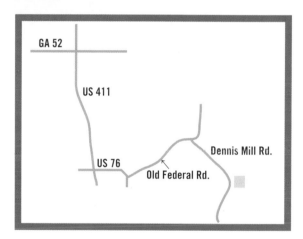

DRIVING DIRECTIONS

From the intersection of GA 52 and US 76/US 411/GA 61, go south on US 411 for 5.3 miles. Turn left on US 76 East. After 0.2 mile, turn left on Old Federal Road South. Go 1.1 miles to Dennis Mill Road. Turn right and drive 0.6 mile. The mill is on the left, just before crossing Rock Creek.

HISTORY

The mill is at the center of what was once the thriving community of Dennis. The community had a general store, post office, tannery, blacksmith shop, cotton gin, and the gristmill. The mill is all that remains.

The community was named after one of the owners of the mill—Dennis Johnson. Some records indicate that a mill at this location dates as far back as 1845. Property records show that James Ramsey purchased the property in 1845. In 1848, he sold it to Charlie Durham, who operated it with John Hawkins as the Hawkins Mill.

The present mill, which Johnson likely built in 1869, remained operational until the 1950s. According to an 1880 census, the mill operated year-round, grinding over 4,200 bushels of wheat and 408,000 pounds of cornmeal. The Hix family, who purchased the mill in 1944, replaced the rotting wooden wheel with a 20-foot steel wheel. Recently Rick and Angie Hix took full ownership of the mill, stabilized it, and built a cabin upstream.

The mill is not open to the public but can be seen from the road. The Hixes have made considerable improvements to the cabins on the property. The cabins are available for rent, providing a family an opportunity to relax and explore trails and the mill on 70 acres along Rock Creek. Online contact can be made at: http://www.vrbo.com/43288.

Berry College Mill

4 *Berry College Mill*

Powered by: Overshot wheel

Water body: Beech Creek/Berry Reservoir

2277 Martha Berry Highway NW, Mount Berry 30149

706-232-5374

www.berry.edu

N34 19 29.5 W85 14 57.6

Tourism Region: Historic High Country

Views of Berry College Mill

DRIVING DIRECTIONS

Traveling westbound on US 411, turn right (north) on East Rome Bypass (Rome Loop 1). Drive 8.4 miles. Take a right at the light on Martha Berry Highway (US 27N). Drive 0.7 mile and turn left into Berry College's main entrance. Follow signs to the mill.

Note: do not use the GPS coordinates until you enter the college campus.

HISTORY

Berry College Mill was constructed in 1930. The Republic Mining and Manufacturing Company donated the iron hub. The mill was originally located near the village of Shannon, between Rome and Calhoun. Henry Ford had the donated iron hub moved to Berry College, where students rebuilt the wheel. At 42 feet in diameter, this is one of the nation's largest overshot waterwheels. Berry Reservoir Lake supplies water to the wheel. The wheel is turned by gravity pushing water up the stone column and over the wheel.

During 1985, physical plant staff and student volunteers restored the mechanism and made grinding of cornmeal once again possible. The mill is operated on special occasions such as Mountain Day. When available, the Oak Hill Gift Shop sells cornmeal ground at the mill.

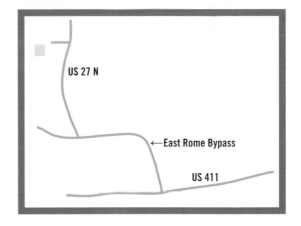

US 27 N

←East Rome Bypass

US 411

Old Brick Mill in Lindale

5 Old Brick Mill in Lindale aka Hoss Mill aka Barnett's Mill aka Jones's Mill

Powered by: Overshot wheel

Water body: Silver Creek

Closest address to the mill:

102 Park Avenue, Lindale 30161

N34 11 17.2 W85 10 25.9

Tourism Region: Historic High Country

Old Brick Mill in Lindale

DRIVING DIRECTIONS

Driving westbound on US 411 South towards Rome, take the Maple Road Exit and turn left. After 2.4 miles, the road becomes Park Avenue. The mill is on the left after 0.2 mile.

HISTORY

In 1832, slave labor constructed the Old Brick Mill in Lindale using bricks made from clay quarried near the site. Larkin Barnett was the first owner. In 1840, flour from the mill was sent to the Paris World Fair where it won first place. During the Civil War, Union soldiers damaged the mill, but Captain Jack Hoss eventually restored it. The mill was listed on the National Register of Historic Places in 1993.

The gristmill is across the street from the ruins of an industrial textile mill that was closed in 2001 and dismantled in 2004. The Pepperell Textile Mill (originally Massachusetts Mill) is sometimes referred to as the Lindale Mill. It is currently marketed as a small-to-large production and film location. It was used as a site for the movie *Allegiant*.

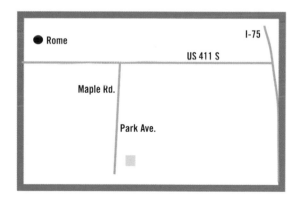

Euharlee Covered Bridge

6 Euharlee Covered Bridge

Construction type: Town's Lattice Truss

Water body: Euharlee Creek

116 Covered Bridge Road SW, Euharlee 30120

770-607-2017

www.euharleehistory.org

Hours: Bridge is open 7 days a week; museum next
   door is open Wed.-Sat., 10 AM-5 PM; SUN., 1-5 PM

N34 08 33.7 W84 55 51.1

Tourism Region: Historic High Country

Euharlee Covered Bridge with the foundation of the gristmill in foreground

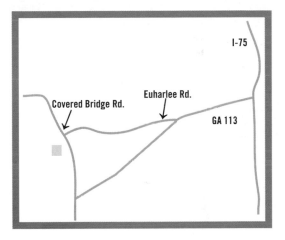

DRIVING DIRECTIONS

From 1-75 near Cartersville, take Exit 288 and proceed south on GA 113 about 4.5 miles. Turn right on Euharlee Road. Go 5.5 miles and turn left onto Covered Bridge Road. Go 0.5 mile and the turn right into the museum parking lot.

HISTORY

The origin of the name *Euharlee* comes from a Creek word meaning "she laughs." The area where this covered bridge is located was originally settled as early as 1808. The area really began to grow in the 1840s when the gristmill began operation. The small settlement was known as Burgess or Burgess Mill. It was incorporated as Euharlee in 1870. The mill, of which only the foundation remains, was sold to Daniel Lowry.

In 1886, Bartow County contracted with Washington W. King, son of freed slave and noted bridge-builder Horace King, and Jonathan H. Burke for the construction of this 138-foot bridge. (You can read more about Horace King's impressive life in the Southwest section under the Red Oak Covered Bridge entry.) The bridge uses the Town's Lattice Truss design—timbers crisscrossing at 45- and 60-degree angles, joined by wooden pegs. This was the third bridge built in this location. The first collapsed and the second was destroyed by flood.

The area warrants a visit because the bridge is the centerpiece of a small tourist area, which includes a vintage 1850s general store, the Euharlee Welcome Center and History Museum, and picnic grounds.

Gresham's Mill

7 Gresham's Mill aka Sixes Mill

Powered by: Overshot wheel

Water body: Toonigh Creek

Approximate address: 964 Sixes Road, Canton 30114

Facebook: Gresham's Mill

N34 09 02.5 W84 31 07.6

Tourism Region: Historic High Country

Gresham's Mill

DRIVING DIRECTIONS

Driving northbound on I-575, take Exit 11 for Sixes Road. Turn left or westbound and proceed about 0.2 mile. The mill is on the right as you cross Toonigh Creek.

HISTORY

The original mill, which was located on the west side of the creek, was built circa 1878-80. It was known as Robert's Mill. Prior to the Land Lottery of 1832, which dispensed the land formerly held by Cherokees, the area was reportedly mined for gold. In 1838, the land was the site of a Georgia militia encampment during the Cherokee Removal.

In the mid-1960s, Lewis Gresham purchased the property and moved the mill across the creek. He began restoring the property with the intent of resuming milling. Gresham also collected many antiques that are in storage at the mill and on his property upstream from the mill. The mill is on private land so you can only observe from the road.

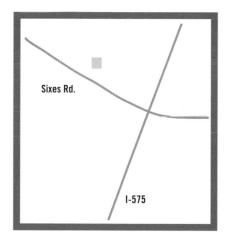

The Old Mill

8 The Old Mill aka Benedicts Mill

Powered by: Overshot wheel
Water body: Little Cedar Creek
12 Old Mill Road, Cedartown 30125
770-712-2949 (Ann Madden)
www.theoldmillvenue.com
Facebook: The Old Mill Venue
N33 58 48.5 W85 15 23.8
Tourism Region: Historic High Country

A close-up of the overshot wheel. The machinery is supposedly still in the mill building, but the wheel hasn't turned in decades.

DRIVING DIRECTIONS

At the intersection of US 278 (M. L. King Blvd.) and US 27 Business (South Main Street) in Cedartown, go south on US 27 Business for 1.2 miles. Follow US 27 Business as it passes over US 27/GA 100 and loops to intersect US 27/GA 100. Turn left on US 27/GA 100 and travel 0.6 mile to Old Mill Road. Turn left and the mill is on the right.

HISTORY

This mill was built in 1848 by slave labor for Asa Prior, who came to Polk County in 1837. It was operated as a mill until 1960, when it was converted to a restaurant, which remained in business until 1991. In 1997, new owners converted it into a private residence and an antique store It is not open to the public but can be seen from the road. As of spring 2016, the mill was being converted to an event venue.

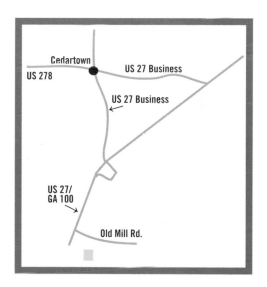

Pine Mountain Gold Mine Mill

C. P. Huntington train is part of the museum's attractions.

Steam-engine display at the stamp-mill section of the gold museum

9 Pine Mountain Gold Mine Mill

Powered by: Overshot wheel

Body of water: N/A

1881 Stockmar Road, Villa Rica 30180

770-459-8455

www.pinemountaingoldmuseum.com

Hours: Mon.-Sat., 10 AM-4 PM; Sun., 1-4 PM

N 33 45 08.4 W84 53 06.3

Tourism Region: Historic High Country

Pine Mountain Gold Mine Mill

DRIVING DIRECTIONS

Traveling west on I-20, take Exit 26 (Liberty Road). Turn north and go 1.3 miles until the road ends at GA 61. Turn right and go 0.2 mile to Stockmar Road. Turn right and go 1.2 miles. The park is on the left.

Note: GPS navigation systems often do not work here. It is recommended that you follow the directions above.

HISTORY

The Pine Mountain Gold Mine Mill is in the Pine Mountain Gold Museum at Stockmar Park, which is a part of the Villa Rica Parks and Recreation Department. The mill was built in the modern era by the parks department. Dan Wooley donated the mill machinery in honor of his grandfather, Zack Barnes, who operated a mill on the Little Tallapoosa River between Carrollton and Tyus, Georgia.

The area is significant because it is arguably the site of the first gold discovery in Georgia. Dahlonega is the better-known area for Georgia gold, but this area is part of a gold belt that extended from Rabun County through Carroll County (Villa Rica), before ending in Alabama. In addition to the mill, the gold museum and park enhances a visit to the area. The C.P. Huntington train takes a scenic trek around the mountain. Visitors can rent equipment to pan for gold and gemstones.

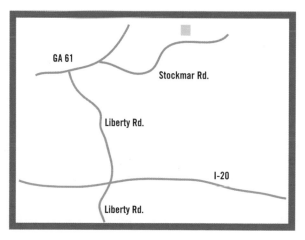

Concord Covered Bridge

Ruff's Mill

10 Concord Covered Bridge and Ruff's Mill

Mill powered by: Turbine

Bridge construction type: Queen Rod Truss with steel (or iron) tension rods

Water body: Nickajack Creek

Concord Road SW, Smyrna 30082

770-933-7228

N33 50 56.8 W84 33 32.6

Tourism Region: Atlanta Metro

Remains of Concord Woolen Mill

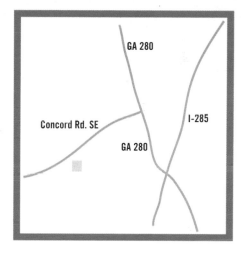

DRIVING DIRECTIONS

From I-285, take Exit 15 south of Smyrna. Turn north on GA 280 and go 4.2 miles to Concord Road SE. Turn left and go 2.4 miles to where the bridge crosses Nickajack Creek.

HISTORY

This 132-foot bridge was built over Nickajack Creek in 1872. It is now part of an historic area. The bridge receives a very high traffic count and there is no good place to park near the bridge, so extreme care is required. It is best to park at the Concord Road Trailhead and walk 0.2 mile to access Heritage Park. The park has a 1.7-mile trail, which was an old railroad bed now converted to a dedicated hiking and biking trail along the creek. It passes the ruins of the Concord Woolen Mill, gives access to the Concord Covered Bridge, and passes by Ruff's Mill.

The Concord Woolen Mill, which first opened in 1847, made Confederate uniforms during the Civil War.

It was burned by Sherman's troops in 1864. It was rebuilt but destroyed by fire again in 1889. It was rebuilt again, but later abandoned in 1916 and has since deteriorated. The Georgia Department of Transportation has stabilized the walls of the mill and dye house.

Ruff's Mill is located next to the bridge. Originally built by William Daniel in the 1840s, it was purchased by the Ruff family in 1855. The surrounding area was the site of a Civil War battle on July 4, 1864. The mill, which is now located on private property, is in a state of disrepair.

Lefler Mill

The walkway to the rear of the mill

A cob barn, part of the nineteenth-century village

11 Lefler Mill aka Pine Run Mill aka Life University Gristmill

Powered by: Overshot wheel

Water body: Rottenwood Creek

1269 Barclay Circle, Marietta 30060

770-426-2600

www.life.edu

N33 55 56.7 W84 30 59.3

Tourism Region: Atlanta Metro

Lefler Mill

DRIVING DIRECTIONS

Traveling on I-75 south of Marietta, take Exit 261. Go westbound on GA 280 South/Delk Road. Merge onto Spinks Drive and turn right onto GA 3/US 41. After 0.5 mile, turn left onto Barclay Circle. The mill is on the left in the Nineteenth-Century Historic Village, just prior to the skywalk on the campus of Life University. Stop at the security office to get a parking permit to visit the mill site.

HISTORY

The mill is on the campus of Life University, a private university that offers undergraduate programs and graduate programs in the health and wellness fields. It is also known for its Doctor of Chiropractic program.

The mill was originally built circa 1884. It was purchased from J. T. Lefler, owner of the Pine Run Mill in Hillsville, Virginia. At one time, it was converted to run on power from an automobile engine. Once transported and rebuilt on this campus, it was restored to its original water-powered specifications. It is located on the former site of the Sewell Mill, which was built in the 1830s. That mill burned many years ago.

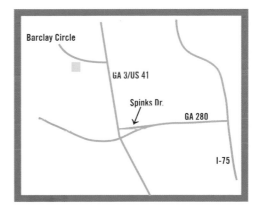

The current mill, which includes the millstones, wooden gears, and the building from the Pine Run Mill, was last operated 50 years ago. The mill is part of the campus's Nineteenth-Century Historic Village, a collection of actual nineteenth-century structures, which includes the mill, cabins, a blacksmith shop, and barns.

Ragsdale Mill

PART II

The Northeast

The Northeast region starts in the northeast corner of Georgia and spreads westward. The mountains in this area are part of the Blue Ridge Mountains, a chain in the Appalachian Mountains system.

The highest point in Georgia—Brasstown Bald at 4,784 feet—is found in this area. The region is known for its stunning scenery and rushing rivers and streams, which provide many possible locations for gristmills. This section of the book includes seventeen gristmills and five covered bridges.

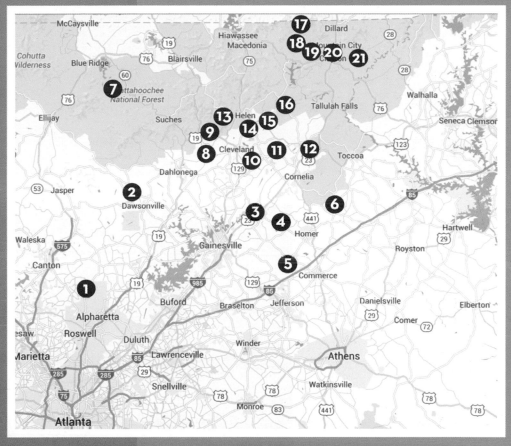

Poole's Mill Covered Bridge

Shoals below Poole's Mill Covered Bridge

1 Poole's Mill Covered Bridge

Construction type: Town's Lattice Truss

Water body: Settendown Creek

7725 Poole's Mill Road, Ball Ground 30107

770-781-2215 (Forsyth County offices)

N34 17 27.1 W84 14 32.2

Tourism Region: Northeast Georgia Mountains

DRIVING DIRECTIONS

Traveling on GA 400/US 19 north of Cumming, take Exit 16. Go 10.6 miles on GA 369 to Pooles Mill Road. Turn left. The bridge is 0.9 mile on the right.

HISTORY

Circa 1820, Cherokee chief George Welch constructed a gristmill, sawmill, and bridge at this site. In 1838, the Cherokees were removed and forced west on the "Trail of Tears" march. John Maynard of Jackson County won the land in the land lottery and sold it to Jacob Scudder. After his death in 1870, Scudder's heirs sold to Dr. M. L. Pool, who then added a cotton gin to the property in 1880. The spelling of the family name has changed to Poole over time. The family ran the mill until 1947, when they abandoned the property. The mill burned in 1959. The original bridge that stood at this site was washed away in a flood in 1899. In 1902, Bud Gentry built the current bridge, which is 94.6 feet long and 14.5 feet wide. Built using the Town's Lattice Truss design, the bridge has holes that were drilled in the wrong location by the original builders. The project was then abandoned, and Bud Gentry took over the construction. If you look carefully, you can still see the misplaced holes. A revitalization effort began in 1990. The bridge was stabilized with a new

Interior shot showing the open Town's Lattice Truss design

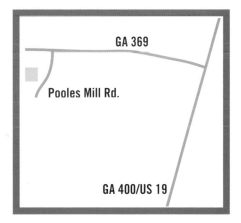

middle pier, new weatherboarding, and a new shingle roof. With the improvements, Poole's Mill Park, which is maintained by Forsyth County Parks & Recreation, was established and is now open to the public. The bridge is closed to vehicles but is open to foot traffic.

Cotton-gin building, located about 50 yards from the mill

The rock pillar built to carry the wooden flume over the creek

2 *Howser Mill aka Dawsonville Mills*

Powered by: Turbine

Water body: Shoal Creek

1000 Howser Mill Road, Dawsonville 30534

N34 25 43.8 W84 08 15.7

Tourism Region: Northeast Georgia Mountains

A winter day at Howser Mill

DRIVING DIRECTIONS

At the intersection of GA 9 and GA 53 in Dawsonville, go west on GA 53 for 0.3 mile to Howser Mill Road. Make a slight right turn onto Howser Mill Road and proceed 1.0 mile. The mill is on the right immediately before crossing Shoal Creek.

HISTORY

Henry Howser came to Dawsonville in 1838 to mine for gold. He and others mined on what is now the Lockheed property and hauled dirt to Shoal Creek for washing and concentration. Most of the miners moved on to California for the 1849 rush, but Henry stayed. In 1866-67, Henry, his brother Thomas, and Josephus Castleberry built the Howser Mill and a cotton gin. One-half mile away, they built a dam on Shoal Creek and a ditch to deliver water to the mill. Two large rock pillars, which can still be seen, were built to carry the wooden flume over the creek. Eventually Thomas became the sole owner. He continued to operate the mill until his death in 1916. Circa 1918, his son Robert converted the turbine wheel of the mill to an electrical power plant and provided power to Dawsonville. In 1938, he sold the power plant to Georgia Power. The dam and flume were dismantled in 1939. The mill, cotton gin, and surrounding land remain in the family and can be seen from alongside the road.

Howser Mill Rd.

GA 53

Dawsonville GA 9

*Abandoned home across
the road from Healan Mill*

3 *Healan Mill aka Head's Mill*

Powered by: Overshot wheel

Water body: North Oconee River

5770 Whitehall Road, Lula 30554

N34 21 55.7 W83 43 54.0

Tourism Region: Northeast Georgia Mountains

DRIVING DIRECTIONS

Where northbound I-985 merges with US 23 (Cornelia Highway) near New Holland, go north on US 23 for 4.1 miles. Turn right on Whitehall Road. Travel 0.2 mile and turn left to stay on Whitehall Road. The mill is 0.4 mile on the left.

HISTORY

Built by William Head in 1852, this mill was originally known as Head's Mill. During the Great Depression, the metal waterwheel replaced the original wooden wheel. By 1945, electricity and general goods were available, making the mill obsolete. By the 1960s, the mill was in shambles when it was sold to Fred and Burnice Healan. It was placed on the National Register of Historic Places in 1990.

Hall County purchased the mill in 2003 and stabilized it. The county entered into an agreement with Head's Mill Historic Preservation Trust, which had the long-term goal of renovating the mill and converting the nearby area into a park. Many issues arose that prevented these efforts. The mill currently sits behind a chainlink fence, waiting for renovation. Plans for restoration have regained momentum. An advisory committee has formed to restore the mill. With support from the county, the committee hopes to restore the mill to its 1935 appearance.

A close-up of Healan Mill's overshot wheel. It is more visible in the winter when the foliage is at a minimum.

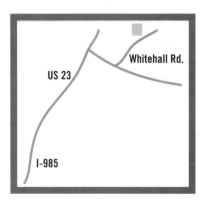

Lula Covered Bridge

4 Lula Covered Bridge

Construction type: King Post

Water body: Grove Creek

Approximate address: 520 Antioch Road, Lula 30554

N34 21 33.8 W83 38 30.3

Tourism Region: Northeast Georgia Mountains

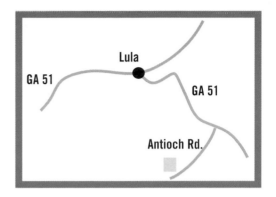

DRIVING DIRECTIONS

From Lula, cross the railroad tracks on Athens Street. Take a slight left on GA 51 and proceed 2.1 miles to Antioch Road. Turn right and go 1.0 mile. The bridge is on the right.

HISTORY

At 34 feet, this bridge has the distinction of being the shortest covered bridge in Georgia and one of the smallest in the country. Originally built in 1915, it was then known as the Hyder Bridge. It was in service until 1969, when the road was shifted, paved, and a new concrete bridge was built to cross the creek. In 1975, the bridge was rebuilt and placed on its original foundations. In the late 2000s, students from Banks County High School renovated the bridge. Unfortunately, the bridge is on private land next to an abandoned golf course and is not accessible to the public. You can glimpse it through the trees as you pass by on Antioch Road.

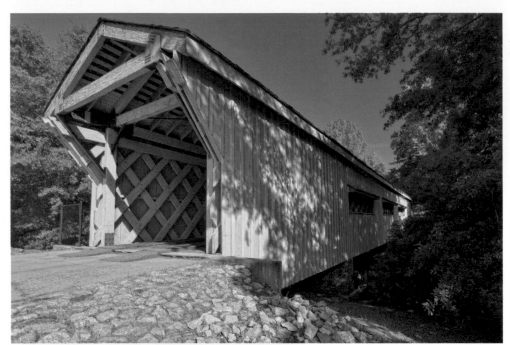

*Hurricane Shoals
Covered Bridge*

A view of the church from a cabin interior at Heritage Village

Cabin and outbuildings at Heritage Village

5 *Hurricane Shoals Mill and Covered Bridge*

Mill powered by: Overshot Wheel

Bridge construction type: Town's Lattice Truss

Water Body: North Oconee River

416 Hurricane Shoals Road, Maysville 30558

706-367-6350

www.hurricaneshoalspark.org

Hours: Closed January & February; see website for hours

N34 12 51.2 W83 32 36.4

Tourism Region: Northeast Georgia Mountains

Hurricane Shoals Mill

DRIVING DIRECTIONS

Traveling northbound on I-85 toward Maysville, take Exit 140. Turn right on Dry Pond Road/GA 82. After 1.9 miles, turn left on GA 82 Connector North. Go 2.2 miles, passing under I-85, to Hurricane Shoals County Park.

HISTORY

The mill began operation in 1870 and continued operations to the mid-1920s. The foundations of the original mill can still be seen on the Jefferson side of the park. In the late 1970s, Hurricane Shoals County Park was established. The gristmill, which was rebuilt in the 1980s, grinds corn today. The original covered bridge was built in 1882 spanning 127 feet. Vandals burned the old bridge in 1972. In 1994, work began to secure funding to rebuild the bridge. In 2002, the new bridge and surrounding paths were formally dedicated. Right before entering the county park is the Heritage Village. The village contains

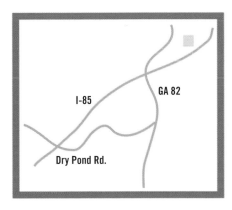

many historical structures from the area, which have been preserved. The buildings include log cabins, a corncrib, a smokehouse, and a chapel.

Overshot wheel

*An old country store located
on the mill property*

6 Ragsdale Mill

Powered by: Overshot wheel
Water body: Ragsdale Creek
697 Mt. Olivet Road, Homer 30547
706-499-3332 or 706-677-3705/2108
N34 23 22.9 W83 25 48.6
Tourism Region: Northeast Georgia Mountains

Ragsdale Mill

DRIVING DIRECTIONS

From Homer, head east on GA 51 toward Athens Street. After 1.4 miles, turn right to stay on GA 51E for 2.7 miles. Turn left on Damascus Road and go 0.5 mile, then make a slight right onto Mt. Olivet Road and go 1.5 miles. The mill is on the east side of the stream.

HISTORY

Reverend Francis Marion Ragsdale originally built the mill in 1863. The millstones were quarried in France and brought into Savannah by blockade runners to bypass the Union navy guarding the port. In 1967, Dr. James and Nancy Cantrell purchased and restored the mill. Circa 2003, the mill was sold to Dock and Nan Sisk. Both Dock and Nan have won the Naismith Women's Official of the Year Award for their college basketball officiating. About 2007, they restored the wheel and flume.

This mill is on private land and is often used for special events and as a wedding venue. In addition to the mill, there are a restored homestead, cabins, and a church on the same grounds.

Many consider this mill one of the more picturesque

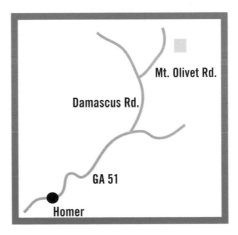

gristmill settings in Georgia. One can arrange for permission to see the grounds by calling Dock or Nan Sisk at one of the telephone numbers listed above or by visiting their home nearby to ask permission.

Skeenah Creek Mill

7 Skeenah Creek Mill

Powered by: Overshot wheel

Water body: Skeenah Creek

20 Skeenah Gap Road, Suches 30572

706-838-5500

www.skeenahcreekcampgroud.com

N34 46 09.1 W84 10 17.5

Tourism Region: Historic High Country

Skeenah Creek Mill

DRIVING DIRECTIONS

From Dahlonega, drive north on GA 60/US 19 for about 30 miles. Turn right onto Skeenah Gap Road. The mill is part of the Skeenah Creek Campground on the right.

HISTORY

In 1838, Willis Rabun Woody traveled with his family from North Carolina and settled in his new home in Fannin County, Georgia. In 1848, he built this mill, which is now located on the grounds of a private campground. On the first floor, rye, wheat, and corn were ground; the second floor was a sawmill. Today, there is a new red steel waterwheel. The mill still operates occasionally.

Lott Mill

8 *Lott Mill*

Powered by: Overshot wheel
Water body: Town Creek
2486 Adair Mill Road, Cleveland 30528
708-219-2076 (Dr. Tom Lott)
N34 36 49.7 W83 51 00.8
Tourism Region: Northeast Georgia Mountains

DRIVING DIRECTIONS

From the courthouse square in Cleveland, go north on GA 11 for 4.8 miles. Turn left on Adair Mill Road and go 2.5 miles. The mill is on the right, just before crossing Town Creek.

HISTORY

Dr. Tom and Joyce Lott own the mill. After Dr. Lott retired, he started a collection of about 20 historic log buildings naming it Cabin in the Laurel–an 1850s Heritage Farm. When Dr. Lott wanted a mill for his collection in 2005, he built one using materials that would age quickly. The mill can be seen from the road or you can call Dr. Lott at 708-219-2076 for permission to enter the property. Dr. Lott is constantly adding to his collection of historic buildings. They are not visible from the road, so to see them you will have to make prior arrangement with Dr. Lott.

Scenes from Cabin in the Laurel–1850s Heritage Farm

Adair Mill

9 Adair Mill

Powered by: Overshot wheel

Water body: Town Creek

55 Mill Creek Trail, Cleveland 30528

N34 37 32.5 W83 50 39.6

Tourism Region: Northeast Georgia Mountains

DRIVING DIRECTIONS

From the courthouse square in Cleveland, go north on GA 11 for 4.8 miles. Turn left on Adair Mill Road. Go 1.1 miles and veer right on Mill Lane. After 0.2 mile, turn right on Mill Creek Trail. The entrance to the mill is on the left.

HISTORY

Adair Mill was built in the mid-1800s. Calvin D. Dalton, who purchased the property in 1996, built a home and rebuilt the mill building. The overshot wheel has been removed but internal gearing and the millstones are still in place. The building has been modernized with good flooring, walls, and lighting. Dalton now rents the building and grounds for small weddings and events. The milldam and well-maintained grounds contribute to a very attractive setting.

The millstone in the interior of Adair Mill

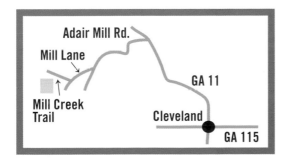

Johnson Mill

Johnson Mill's overshot wheel. Note the wooden construction of the wheel. The main shaft is carved from a tree trunk.

The small covered non-historical bridge across the highway from the mill

10 Johnson Mill

Powered by: Overshot wheel

Water body: Branch of Mossy Creek

226 Cooley Woods Road, Cleveland 30528

706-865-4848

N34 34 45.6 W83 43 26

Tourism Region: Northeast Georgia Mountains

An interior view of the mill. Note the millstones.

DRIVING DIRECTIONS

From Cleveland, go 1.9 miles east on GA 115. Turn right on Black Road and go 0.7 mile. Turn right on Cooley Woods Road. The mill is on the right.

HISTORY

Johnson Mill was originally built in the late-1880s and was restored by Gordon Pfau. Ray Payne now owns it. The mill is notable because the solid wood shaft, carved from a single tree trunk, drives the huge wooden waterwheel. Historically, early mill wheels and shafts were constructed of wood; this is one of the few mills left with this construction.

After restoration, the mill was fully operational, but it hasn't operated in some time. Since all the equipment is still in the mill, it might be easy to make it operational again. The mill site has a small lake in the foreground and a quintessential cabin on the property. The owners welcome visitors with a prior appointment. Their phone number is 706-865-4848. If you don't have an appointment, the mill and adjacent buildings are readily visible from the road.

The mill entrance with a small cabin in the background

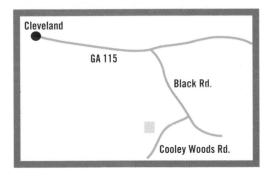

Pardue Mill

11 *Pardue Mill aka Perdue Mill*

Powered by: **Overshot wheel**

Water body: **Yellowbank Creek**

722 Pardue Mill Road, Cleveland 30528

N34 35 32.8 W83 35 07

Tourism Region: **Northeast Georgia Mountains**

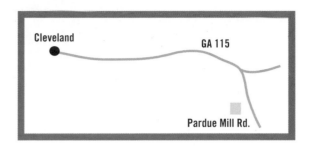

DRIVING DIRECTIONS

From Cleveland, go 10.6 miles east on GA 115. Turn right on Pardue Mill Road and go 0.5 mile. The mill is on the right.

HISTORY

Pardue, also called Perdue, Mill was originally built in the 1930s. It stayed operational until the mid-1960s. The owner built the mill, a barn on a hill above the mill, and a house between the mill and the road. The house no longer stands but the mill and barn remain. The milldam, located above a cascading waterfall, is in excellent condition. Although the mill is on private property, there is a nice view from the road.

Close up of where the overshot wheel was

Laudermilk Mill

12 | *Laudermilk Mill aka Short's Mill*

Powered by: Overshot wheel

Water body: Hazel Creek

3240 GA 197, Mt. Airy 30563

N34 34 06.6 W83 29 32

Tourism Region: Northeast Georgia Mountains

Laudermilk Mill

DRIVING DIRECTIONS

From the south part of Clarkesville, where US 441 Business/GA 197/GA 115/GA 17 all run conjunctively at Washington Street, go south on GA 197 for 2.7 miles. Shortly before coming to US 23/US 441, cross Hazel Creek. The mill is on the left.

HISTORY

The mill, which was built by Tom Laudermilk in 1880, ceased operation in 1975. In addition to the gristmill, there was a shingle mill on the ground floor. During its heyday in the early 1900s, owner Homer Ansley processed 75 bushels of meal a day here. The grounds, cascading stream, and mill combine for a charming setting. Although the mill is on private land, there is a nice view of the structure from the road. The chase is gone and the main mill structure needs major reinforcement. The mill parts are still there, but they need to be restored and rebuilt. A foundation was formed to spearhead attempts to restore the mill. In the fall of 2015, the mill and adjacent property went up for sale, but the foundation still hopes to purchase and restore it.

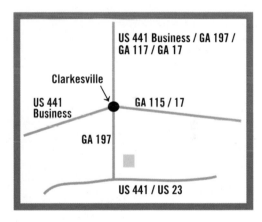

Bay's Bridge

13 Bay's Bridge

Construction type: Modern
Water body: Dukes Creek
61 Tsalaki Trail, Helen 30545
706-878-3087
www.gastateparks.org
Hours: 8 AM-5 PM daily
N34 41 30.1 W83 46 09.4
Tourism Region: Northeast Georgia Mountains

Bay's Bridge

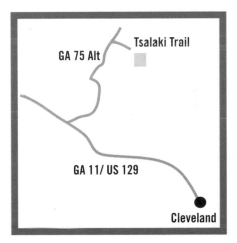

DRIVING DIRECTIONS

From Cleveland, drive north on GA 11/US 129 for 3.3 miles. At GA 75 Alt, turn right and proceed 5.7 miles to Tsalaki Trail and enter Smithgall Woods State Park/ Dukes Creek Conservation Area. If you come from Helen, the park entrance is 3.0 miles west on GA 75 Alt. The GPS coordinates are the entrance to the state park.

HISTORY

Strictly speaking, this is actually not a historical bridge, but it is included because of its location in the Smithgall Woods State Park. The park offers premier fishing and retreat facilities. From the visitor center, Tsalaki Trail serves as an access road to property owners and the central part of the park. Not normally open to vehicular traffic, the bridge is reached by an easy 1.5-mile hike on Tsalaki Trail. Along the hike, you can enjoy spectacular mountain woods, streamside hiking, and access to a short wetland loop trail for observing waterfowl, frogs, and other wildlife.

Fly fishing in the waters of the Chattahoochee River next to Nora Mill

Bevel gears transfer the power of the turbine (out of sight below this image) to the interior main shaft wheel. Note that the horizontal bevel gear teeth are made of wood. This gear undergoes considerable stress, so the teeth wear out quickly. It is more economical to change the wooden teeth as required than to replace a solid-steel bevel gear.

Bevel gears below the milldam. The turbine is below the bevel gears.

The wooden bar, which is about 2 x 2 inches against the split vertical bar, is known as the damsel. As the millstone spins, the bar rocks the bin to feed the corn into the millstone opening. An experienced miller can listen to the sound of the vibration and tell when the feed rate is just right. If the speed is incorrect and the corn feed rate is off, the miller can judge the "damsel is in distress" and make the necessary adjustments.

14 *Nora Mill*

Powered by: Turbine
Water body: Chattahoochee River
7107 South Main Street, Helen 30545
706-878-2375
www.noramill.com
Hours: Mon.-Sat., 9 AM-5 PM; Sun., 10 AM-5 PM
N34 41 22.9 W83 42 40
Tourism Region: Northeast Georgia Mountains

Nora Mill

DRIVING DIRECTIONS

From the Chattahoochee River Bridge in the town of Helen, go S/SE on GA 75/GA 17 for 1.2 miles. The mill is on the left.

HISTORY

Dan Brown built the original mill on the site in 1824. John Martin came to Georgia to mine for gold but instead settled in the Sautee-Nacoochee Valley and built the current mill in 1876. It has a wooden dam and a 100-foot raceway that powers the turbine. It was sold to a Captain Nicholas and later to a Mr. Honecut. In 1902, the future governor of Georgia, Dr. Lamartine G. Hardman, purchased the property and renamed it Nora Mill in memory of his sister.

In the early 1980s, retired Army lieutenant colonel Ron Fain leased the mill from the Hardman family and restored the stone milling operation. He became the miller, working alongside his parents until their passing, and then worked with his youngest daughter Joann, as she learned the art of milling and how to manage the business. In 1998, a group of investors headed by Tom

Flick purchased the Hardman holdings, including the gristmill building. They developed Nacoochee Village, which surrounds the area today. The village includes several businesses, including the Habersham Vineyard & Winery, restaurants, and shops.

Today, Ron's daughter Joann Fain Tarpley and her husband retain ownership of all the milling equipment but lease the gristmill building as part of the Nacoochee Village. Their son, Joe Vandegriff, manages the gristmill operation, producing fresh grains for sale throughout the year. Tommy Martin is the current miller. If he isn't busy operating the mill, he is delighted to spend time discussing the art of the milling process.

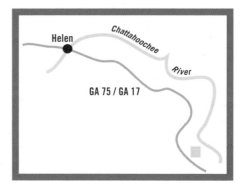

Stovall Bridge

15 *Stovall Bridge*

Construction type: Queen Post
Water body: Chickamauga Creek
Along old Clayton Highway (GA 255),
   near 12 Rau Road,
   Sautee Nacoochee 30571
N34 42 41.5 W83 39 27.5
Tourism Region: Northeast Georgia
   Mountains

Stovall Bridge

DRIVING DIRECTIONS

From Cleveland, drive north toward Helen on GA 75 to Nacoochee. Turn right on GA 17. Pass the old Sautee General Store, and turn left on GA 255. The bridge is on the right.

HISTORY

At 36.8 feet, this is the shortest clear-span covered bridge in Georgia. Fred Dover, who also owned a gristmill, sawmill, and shingle mill as well as other businesses in the area, built the original bridge at this location. After the bridge was destroyed by flood, Will Pardue built the present bridge in 1895. In 1917, Fred Stovall purchased the bridge and businesses, which no longer exist. Today, picnic facilities and a parking area are near the bridge.

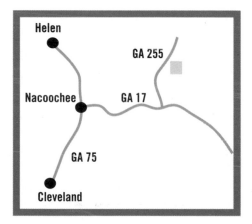

View of the Soque River from the balcony of the mill

Interior view of the mill, which shows a pottery display and information stand.

A view from underneath the mill, showing the turbine and shaft that power the main drive wheel

16 Mark of the Potter Mill aka Grandpa Watts Mill

Powered by: Wooden turbine (tub wheel)

Water body: Soque River

9982 GA 197 North, Clarkesville 30523

706-947-3440

www.markofthepotter.com

Hours: Jan-March; 10 AM-5 PM; April-Dec., 10 AM-6 PM

N34 43 46.1 W83 35 20

Tourism Region: Northeast Georgia Mountains

Mark of the Potter Mill

DRIVING DIRECTIONS

At the intersection of GA 385 and GA 197 in Clarkesville, go north on GA 197 for 9.9 miles. The mill is on the right.

HISTORY

When the Cherokees were forced to cede their lands in 1817, this site was distributed in the fourth land lottery of 1820. Isaac and William Daniel Hill operated separate mills, which were called the Hills Mills. One of these mills was built on this site in the 1820s.

In 1928, Alan and Robert Watts, a father and son team of millers, bought the mill with the intention that Robert would run this mill while "Grandpa" Alan would continue running the family's other mills. The current building was built in 1931, adjacent to one of the old Hills Mills. At one time, there was an old gristmill upstream, a sawmill at the present location, and a furniture factory downstream. All were driven by waterpower from the Soque River. The Soque River, which was dammed upstream, provided water to a 10,000-gallon penstock, de-livering the water pressure to drive the tub wheel/turbine.

In 1969, John and Glen LaRowe decided to open a pottery shop. They found the old Grandpa Watts gristmill, which had been closed due to flooding. After acquiring the property, they repaired the buildings and set up a studio. The mill building is now a pottery shop where the current owners endeavor to provide the best functional stoneware from potters on site and from specially selected potters throughout the country. The owners have kept the historical nature of the building. On the main floor, along with the pottery, one can see much of the mill's workings. The present building is driven by a tub wheel/turbine, which can still be seen via a small passageway below the pottery area. The lower level of the building provides the opportunity to view the tub wheel/turbine, shafts, and pulleys. The mill is open to the public during business hours. On the route to the mill, the drive along the Soque River on Scenic Highway GA 197 offers one of the more beautiful drives in Georgia.

Barker's Creek Mill

The mill raceway

17 *Barker's Creek Mill*

Powered by: Overshot wheel

Water body: Barker's Creek

Betty's Creek Road, Rabun Gap 30568

706-746-5718

www.hambridge.org/the-mill

N34 59 30 W83 26 34.8

Tourism Region: Northeast Georgia Mountains

Barker's Creek Mill

DRIVING DIRECTIONS

From the intersection of US 23 and US 76 in Clayton, go north 6.7 miles on US 23 to Betty's Creek Road. Turn left, and go 4.4 miles to a pullout on the left. Park here and walk on an old road about 200 yards to the mill. Pass Hambridge Center for the Creative Arts & Sciences on the way to the mill.

HISTORY

Barker's Creek Mill has provided milling services to the local community since the mid-1800s. Mary Hambridge built the current mill in 1944 on the site of an older mill. The mill is powered by a 12-foot overshot wheel set on babbet bearings. The mill itself is a vertical mill with two 16-inch flint/granite stones. It was built by the Meadow's Milling Company in North Wilkesboro, North Carolina. The mill is part of the Hambridge Center for the Creative Arts & Sciences, a residency program to help artists develop and express their creative voices. The entrance to the Hambridge Center is about 0.8 mile before reaching the turnout to the mill. The first Saturday of each month, the mill provides grinding services to local

farmers. Grits and cornmeal, which are stone ground by the mill, are sold in the Hambridge Center's Weave Shed Gallery or at the mill on the first Saturday of each month.

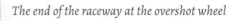
The end of the raceway at the overshot wheel

The view upstream from the mill. The milldam is in the background. The raceway is in the upper right corner.

18 *Dickerson Mill*

Powered by: Overshot wheel

Water body: Keener Creek

10 Water Wheel Lane, Rabun Gap 30568

N34 56 14.6 W83 26 35

Tourism Region: Northeast Georgia Mountains

Dickerson Mill

DRIVING DIRECTIONS

At the intersection of US 76W and US 23/US 441 in Clayton, go north on US 441 for 4.2 miles. Turn left on Wolffork Road. Go 4.4 miles and turn left on Blue Ridge Gap Road. Go 300 feet to Water Wheel Lane. The mill is on the left.

HISTORY

In 1926, Bill Dickerson built the mill on Keener Creek. The same waterwheel here today was used to run the gristmill and a sawmill. Alan and Elaine Nelson purchased the property, converted it into a residence, and landscaped the surrounding property. The dam is located about 200 feet upstream from the property. A flume transports the water to the wheel. Around 2002, the property was sold to Jay Cunningham. Now, it is maintained as a private residence. The dam, landscaping, wooden walkways, and gazebos make for a beautiful mountain setting, but please respect the property and do not enter it.

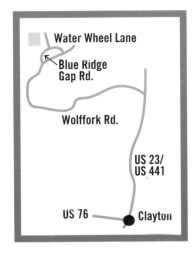

Sylvan Falls Mill

19 *Sylvan Falls Mill*

Powered by: Overshot wheel

Water body: Pit Branch

156 Taylors Chapel Road, Rabun Gap 30568

706-746-7138

www.sylvanfallsmill.com

Hours: 10 AM-6 PM

N34 55 38.4 W83 25 13.8

Tourism Region: Northeast Georgia Mountains

Winter at Sylvan Falls Mill

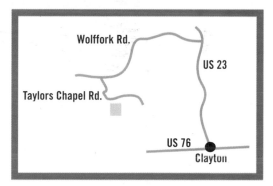

DRIVING DIRECTIONS

From the intersection of US 23 and US 76 in Clayton, go north 4.2 miles on US 23 to Wolffork Road. Turn left. Go 2.2 miles to Taylors Chapel Road. Turn left. The mill is on the right after 0.2 mile.

HISTORY

The mill, which was constructed in 1840, operated as a gristmill for over 170 years. The original wooden waterwheel was replaced in 1952 by a 27-foot, 10,000-pound steel wheel, which was relocated from Tennessee. The waterfall cascading beside the mill is fed from springs on Black Rock Mountain. Today the mill is a charming bed-and-breakfast with four guest rooms. The innkeepers are Mike and Linda Johnson, who have owned the mill since 2001. The Johnsons still operate the mill to provide fresh ground flour and grist for their own use and for sale to the public.

The sluice system at top of the overshot wheel

The interior of the mill with a close-up of the original wooden gearing

Wagon Shed: This structure originally stood a few miles from Mountain City, Georgia. It is home to the Zuraw Wagon, the only documented wagon known to have traveled to Oklahoma on the Trail of Tears. It also houses the Judd Nelson Wagon, built under commission in 1983, as an educational project for Foxfire students.

Savannah House: Originally from Jackson County, North Carolina, this cabin was built in the 1820s. Foxfire relocated the structure to its present location in 1975.

Interior of the chapel: The interior paneling in the chapel is wormy chestnut, from the nearly extinct American chestnut tree.

The chapel: Unable to locate a local community chapel that the residents would sell or donate, Foxfire constructed this chapel, modeling it after a church that stood in Waynesville, North Carolina.

20 Bell Mill

Powered by: Overshot wheel

Water body: Not Applicable

705 Cross Street, Mountain City 30562

706-746-5828

www.foxfire.org

Hours: Mon-Sat., 8:30 AM-4:30 PM

N34 54 44 W83 23 44

(*Note:* Using GPS is not recommended, as reception is spotty and will misroute you.)

Tourism Region: Northeast Georgia Mountains

Bell Mill

DRIVING DIRECTIONS

From Clayton, go north on US 23/US 441 and watch for the brown signs directing you to Black Rock Mountain State Park. Follow the signs to Black Rock Mountain Parkway and turn left. Travel approximately 1.0 mile. Watch for the first small brown Foxfire sign. At the huge "Black Rock Mountain State Park" sign, turn left onto Down Home Lane. Proceed 0.1 mile onto Cross Street and go 0.4 mile to the entrance of the Foxfire Museum and Heritage Center.

HISTORY

The mill is located at the Foxfire Museum and Heritage Center. Foxfire started in 1966 as a project for Rabun County High School English students, who were charged with interviewing local people about pioneer life in the Appalachians. The magazine the students produced resulted in *The Foxfire Book* and its eleven companion volumes that have sold about 9 million copies. The students used the book royalties to establish a living museum, which preserves authentic pioneer structures and offers demonstrations of how life was lived in the pioneer culture of the southern Appalachian Mountains.

C. B. Bell constructed the mill in the 1920s near Coweta, North Carolina. In 1972, the Foxfire Museum relocated it to its present location and restored it to working condition. It was the first log structure reassembled on the property, leading the way to the museum's collection of over 20 log cabins and outbuildings. For a small admission charge, you can walk through the past and find homes, tools, trades, and crafts from an earlier time.

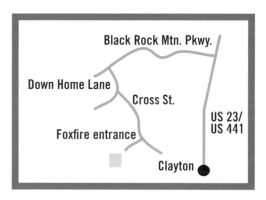

Wilbanks Mill

21 *Wilbanks Mill aka Warwoman Mill aka Darnell Mill*

Powered by: Overshot wheel

Water body: Warwoman Creek

Approximate address: 700 John Houck Road, Clayton 30525

N34 52 59 W83 18 09.3

Tourism Region: Northeast Georgia Mountains

The wooden overshot wheel, which has nearly disappeared

DRIVING DIRECTIONS

At the intersection of US 76 and US 441 in the center of Clayton, turn right on Rickman Drive and go 0.5 mile. Turn right on Warwoman Road and go 5.3 miles. Make a slight right turn on Sandys Ford Road. After 300 feet, turn right again on Sandys Ford Road. Proceed 0.6 mile to the intersection of Sandys Ford and John Houck Roads. There is good parking at this intersection. From the intersection, walk along John Houck Road about 100 yards. Look for the mill on the left on the east bank of the creek.

HISTORY

Unfortunately, this mill is in near ruin. The small mill building has nearly collapsed, only part of the overshot wheel remains, and there is no longer any machinery left. I've included it in this book because it emphasizes the need for mill preservation. This mill was operational in 1980, but today it has nearly disappeared.

The mill was known as Captain Beck's Mill, named for the man who operated it as a sawmill. After his death, there were a series of owners. Later, D.W. (Dixie) Wil-

banks owned the mill. He operated it until 1968. A flooded creek washed it out in 1973. In 1980, it was restored as the Darnell Mill and operated for a few years. Now it is abandoned, and soon there will be little left.

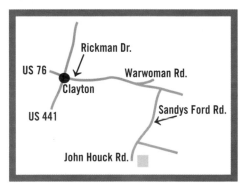

Auchumpkee Creek Covered Bridge

The Southwest region in this book includes the piedmont (the plateau between the coastal plain and Appalachian Mountains) and the coastal plain. It includes the fall line, which is the name for the transitional area between the piedmont and the coastal plain. The name "fall line" refers to the line of rapids and waterfalls that accompany the quick change of elevation from rolling hills to a mostly flat terrain. These rolling hills and accompanying fall line provided the early settlers of Georgia with many ideal locations for gristmills. In this section, there are ten gristmills and three covered bridges.

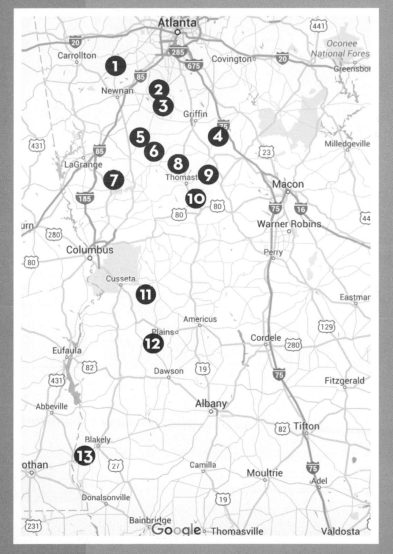

Above: *Looking downstream to the mill*
Right: *A view of the mill interior. The mill is now used by the owner for family events.*

1 *Wilkerson Mill*

Powered by: Overshot wheel

Water body: Little Bear Creek

9595 Wilkerson Mill Road, Chattahoochee Hills 30268

770-463-2400 (Wilkerson Mill Gardens)

www.hydrangea.com

Hours: Closed in winter months; call for hours

N33 33 34.7 W84 42 01

Tourism Region: Atlanta Metro

Wilkerson Mill

DRIVING DIRECTIONS

At the intersection of I-85 and I-285 just west of the Hartsfield-Jackson International Airport in Atlanta, proceed west on South Fulton Parkway. At the intersection of GA 154 (Cascade Palmetto Highway) and South Fulton Parkway, continue westbound on South Fulton Parkway for 2.6 miles to Cochran Mill Road. Turn left onto Cochran Mill Road. After 0.7 mile, turn left onto Wilkerson Mill Road. The entrance to Wilkerson Mill Gardens is on the left after 0.4 mile. The mill is part of this establishment.

HISTORY

The mill, which was built circa 1875, was operational into the 1960s when the competition from self-rising flour forced the miller to shut it down. As the mill went through several owners, it gradually deteriorated. The present owner, Gene Griffin, purchased the property in the 1980s and developed commercial gardens specializing in hydrangeas. Griffin brought in Amish craftsmen to rehabilitate and stabilize the mill. He also put in new flooring and replaced many of the beams. The millstone,

overshot wheel, and gearing still remain, but the owner's objective is to keep the building as is—stable without making any further restoration. The mill is not visible from the road. To see it, enter Wilkerson Mill Gardens during their business hours and ask permission to walk about 100 yards downstream.

Bennett's Mill

2 Bennett's Mill

Powered by: Overshot wheel
Water body: Whitewater Creek
1095 GA 54 W, Fayetteville 30214
770-460-6455
www.franksattheoldmill.com
Hours: Mon.-Sat., 11 AM-10 PM
N33 26 54.6 W84 29 40.1
Tourism Region: Atlanta Metro

Bennett's Mill

DRIVING DIRECTIONS

At the intersection of GA 85 and GA 54 in Fayetteville, go west on GA 54 for 2.3 miles. The mill is on the right.

HISTORY

William Bennett, his wife Lavinia, and their son Cam came to Fayette County in 1823. William built the mill along Whitewater Creek in 1837. The mill, which was run by one 48-horsepower waterwheel, produced 80 bushels of wheat and corn a day at its maximum capacity in 1870. Since its heyday, the mill has served as a community center for picnics and socials, as well as a baptismal site. It was sold in the 1930s. Today, the expanded structure houses Frank's at the Old Mill Mediterranean Grill & Bar.

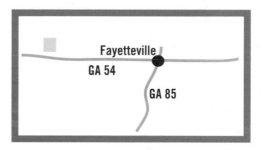

3 Starr's Mill

Powered by: Turbine

Water body: Starrs Millpond on Whitewater Creek

120 Waterfall Way, Fayetteville

770-461-1146

www.fayettecountyga.gov

Hours: 6:30 AM-6 PM

N33 19 45.1 W84 30 30.9

Tourism Region: Atlanta Metro

Starr's Mill

DRIVING DIRECTIONS

At the intersection of GA 85 and GA 54 in Fayetteville, go south on GA 85 for 9.0 miles. The mill is on the right.

HISTORY

Over the years, 16 property owners and three mills have been part of the history of Starr's Mill. Hananiah Gilcoat constructed the original mill in 1825 when his land bordered Creek Territory. It became known as Starr's Mill when Hilliard Starr acquired the property in 1866. After the second mill burned to the ground around 1900, William T. Glower, the property's 13th owner, built the present millhouse in 1907. The mill operated until 1959. It was idle until Fayette County purchased it as a water-system reservoir in 1991. The mill has been featured in many magazines as well as used as a set in the movie *Sweet Home Alabama*. It is now part of a county park, open to the public for fishing

What is believed to be a trail tree is located on private property near the mill. Native Americans throughout the Southeast used these trees to mark trails, stream crossings, or springs. When the trees were saplings, the Indians tied them down for about a year until they grew into a position similar to the tree seen here. The property owner believes this tree was used to mark a nearby spring.

The steps are all that remain of the Chappell home.

Handmade belt-sprocket wheel, located below the mill

4 Chappell's Mill

Powered by: Turbine

Water Body: Buck Creek

Approximate address: 161 Chappell Mill Road, Milner 30257
N33 10 41.5 W84 05 51.3

Tourism Region: Historic Heartland

Note: This mill should not be confused with Chappell's Mill in Laurens County, which is profiled in the Southeast section of this book.

Chappell's Mill

DRIVING DIRECTIONS

Traveling southbound on I-75, take Exit 201. Turn right or west on GA 36. Go 4.0 miles, then turn right on Chappell Mill Road. After 1.2 miles, the mill is on the left, just before crossing Buck Creek.

HISTORY

The Chappell district, which was settled in 1821, was originally named Unionville. In 1921, Lamar County was formed from portions of Pike and Monroe Counties. At that point, the Unionville district courthouse was shut down and a new one was established in the Chappell community. Records are unclear, but it appears Joseph H. English originally built a turbine-powered mill on this site. Eventually, Alfred Chappell, who married English's only daughter, became the mill owner, giving the mill and community its present name. The district supported a general store, a blacksmith shop, a ginnery, schools, several churches, and the mill. Chappell was a prominent businessman, so much is known about his family, but very little is known about the mill itself. It's uncertain exactly when it was built, which member of the English family built it, the production history, or when it ceased operation.

Today, the deteriorating mill can be seen from the bridge over Buck Creek. Only a few surrounding buildings remain. The mill is owned by Keith Morris, who lives nearby. He also owns the Tobler Mill aka Yatesville Mill, covered later in this section of the book.

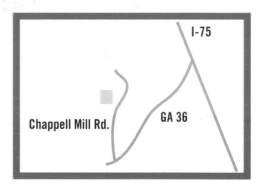

The small structure on the right houses the 125-kilowatt generator, viewed here from below the mill.

Interior view of mill where portions of the original floor have rotted through

Looking back at the mill from below the dam

5 Massengale Mill aka Jones Mill

Powered by: Turbine

Water body: Red Oak Creek

Massengale Mill Road, Gay 30218

N33 04 42.2 W84 36 50.9

Tourism Region: Presidential Pathways

Massengale Mill

DRIVING DIRECTIONS

At the intersection of GA 74 and GA 109 in Gay, go west on GA 109. Proceed 2.3 miles to Massengale Mill Road. Turn right and go 0.3 mile. The mill is on the right.

HISTORY

Around the time Native Americans left the area in 1830, John Jones built a mill on this location with a crib and timber dam, which is now submerged. The present arched concrete dam was built in 1925, along with the present mill. In 1958, Hoke Massengale raised the dam two feet and installed a 125-kilowatt generator to operate a Hammer mill, a steel drum containing a rotating shaft on which hammers are mounted. It is used to crush aggregate material. The mill was last operated circa 1975. In 1994, Forbes Mathews purchased the property. He now operates the generator off grid. One of those interesting oddities of history is that after Mathews purchased the property, he discovered that his great-great grandmother was married to John Jones, the builder of the original mill. The mill building is structurally unsound with just the millstones and hoppers still in the structure. The mill is on private property, but can be seen easily from the road. It is an attraction on the Meriwether–Pike County Scenic Byway.

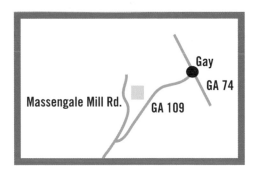

The long timber-decked approach to the bridge

Red Oak Creek Covered Bridge

6 Red Oak Creek Covered Bridge

Construction type: Town's Lattice Truss
Water body: Red Oak Creek
Covered Bridge Road, Woodbury 30293
N33 02 19.0 W84 33 08.6
Tourism Region: Presidential Pathways

DRIVING DIRECTIONS

From the intersection of GA 18 and GA 74 in Woodbury, go north on GA 74 for 2.9 miles. Turn right on Covered Bridge Road and travel 1.2 miles. There is a pull-off area at the western end of the bridge.

HISTORY

This is one of the few remaining bridges constructed by noted bridge-builder Horace King. Born into slavery in 1807, King was mentored by his owner, John Godwin, after Godwin noticed King's extraordinary engineering talents. To allow King greater rights to move about as needed and to own property, the Alabama legislature passed a special act granting him full freedom in the eyes of the law. On his own, he supervised crews of slaves that built bridges across Georgia, Alabama, and Mississippi. This was a remarkable achievement for a freed slave of African-American and Catawba-Indian descent during the antebellum period.

Built in the 1840s, the bridge spans 252.5 feet. It is sometimes known as the Imlac Bridge. The main covered section of the bridge is slightly shorter than that of the Watson Mill Covered Bridge, profiled in the Southeast section of this book. However, with the addition of its wood approach, the Red Oak Creek Covered Bridge is the longest wooden bridge in the state. The central span of

Red Oak Creek Covered Bridge

the bridge, which measures 115 feet, is thought to be the longest unsupported span of any wooden bridge in the state.

The bridge is an attraction on the Meriwether–Pike County Scenic Byway. It was listed on the National Register of Historic Places in 1973.

The west exterior wall is now gone, giving a good view of the overshot wheel and drive system.

A close-up of the overshot wheel and the direct-metal gearing system

A view of the mill from upstream, looking towards the highway

7 | *Hall's Mill*

Powered by: Overshot wheel
Water body: Crawford Creek
Chipley Highway (GA 18), Pine Mountain 31822
N32 53 04.2 W84 50 28.9
Tourism Region: Presidential Pathways

The entire mill is only visible after walking down a heavily over-grown path.

DRIVING DIRECTIONS

At the intersection of US 27 and GA 18 in Pine Mountain, go northeast on GA 18 for 1.5 miles. The mill is on the right, as you cross Crawford Creek. Due to heavy vegetation, the only time you can see the mill from the road is in the winter.

HISTORY

Little is known about the history of this mill. According to SPOOM, the foundation was stabilized circa 2003. The mill has a 21-foot Fitz overshot wheel with 31-inch steel buckets. The building and roof appear in good condition, but parts of the walls are open and exposed to the elements. The area is quite overgrown, making the mill almost impossible to see in the summer. Equipment, belts, and pulleys are still in the building. The mill is on private property, but you can view it from the road.

Hannah's Mill

A view through the door of mill. Note the bevel gears.

8 Hannah's Mill aka Rose Hill Mill

Powered by: Turbine

Water body: Tenmile Creek

1615 Hannahs Mill Road, Thomaston 30286

N32 55 52.6 W84 21 17.

Tourism Region: Presidential Pathways

Hannah's Mill

DRIVING DIRECTIONS

At the intersection of US 19 and Main Street in Thomaston, go west on Main Street (GA 74) for 0.8 mile. Turn right on Hannahs Mill Road. Go 3.7 miles. The mill is on the left.

HISTORY

The mill was constructed in 1859 by Dr. J. W. Herring. It was sold to Dr. G. W. Hannah in 1887. Dr. Herring also reportedly built the nearby Auchumpkee Creek Covered Bridge. In 1935, the McDonald family, who still owns the property, purchased the mill. Originally, the mill had an undershot wheel, which was replaced by a pipe-fed turbine in 1957. On the first floor are two runs of millstones, which are both enclosed in metal encasements. One of the stones is believed to be one of the original 1859 millstones; the other was replaced in the 1930s.

The McDonalds discontinued the commercial milling operation in 1977, but much of the equipment still remains. The present owner, David McDonald, reports that he hopes to eventually resume grinding operations. The mill is on private property, but you can view it from the road.

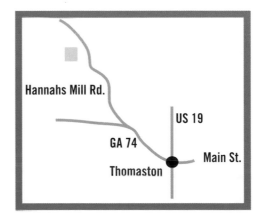

Tobler Mill

Upper right, lower left and right are interior views of the mill.

9 _Tobler Mill aka Hightower Mill aka Yatesville Mill_

Powered by: Overshot wheel

Water body: Tobler Creek

5600 GA 74, Yatesville 31097

N32 55 3.8 W84 10 032.8

Tourism Region: Presidential Pathways

Tobler Mill

DRIVING DIRECTIONS

From Yatesville, go 2.0 miles west on GA 74 (Yatesville Highway). The mill is on the left as you cross Tobler Creek.

HISTORY

The mill's history is traced back to at least 1824, when there was a small settlement at this location. James Hightower owned and operated the mill then. There is convincing evidence that the mill was built earlier—the date September 8, 1792 is inscribed on the original rock foundation. In the 1850s, the McFarlin and Nelson families ran the mill as the Tobler Milling Company. By 1880, it was called the Nelson & Company Mill. It continued operation into the 1950s. After shutting down, it fell into disrepair. The building was barely visible from the road because the area became so overgrown.

In 2003, Bill Browning began restoration of the mill. In 1870, a steel overshot wheel replaced the old wooden wheel. Browning learned that the bulk of the original steel wheel was purchased by a collector in North Carolina. He traveled there, bringing back the 1870s steel wheel, which he restored. The building itself was completely rebuilt, using old photos to replicate the original structure as closely as possible.

Recently, Browning sold the mill to Keith Morris of Lamar County, who also owns the Chappell's Mill ruins noted previously in this section. Morris made further improvements. Today the mill is fully operational and in excellent condition. Although it is on private land, you can observe the mill from the highway.

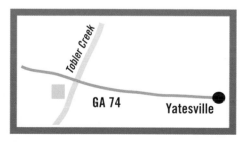

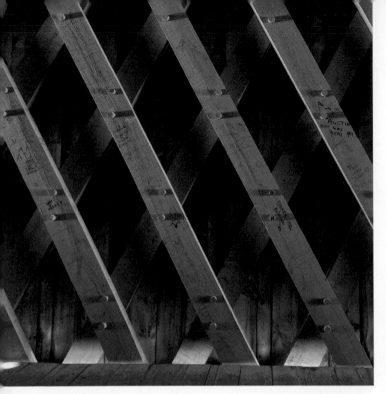

An example of the cross-hatching of Town's Lattice Truss design

A view of the bridge from underneath

10 Auchumpkee Creek Covered Bridge aka Hootenville Bridge

Construction type: Town's Lattice Truss

Water body: Auchumpkee Creek

Allen Road (GA 80), Thomaston 30286

N32 45 19.9 W84 13 47.5

Tourism Region: Presidential Pathways

Auchumpkee Creek Covered Bridge

DRIVING DIRECTIONS

At the intersection of US 19 and Main Street in Thomaston, go south on US 19 for 11.5 miles. Turn left onto Allen Road. Proceed 0.8 mile to the crossing of Auchumpkee Creek. The bridge is on the left. The bridge is not open to traffic. There is a picnic area and parking area at the bridge.

HISTORY

Dr. J. W. Herring designed the 96-foot bridge, which was built by his company (Herring and Alfred) in 1892. In July 1994, tropical storm Alberto dumped 15 inches of rain on this area in one day. A huge tree carried down the raging Auchumpkee Creek knocked the bridge off its moorings. In 1997, federal disaster relief funds and funds raised by a local historic preservation committee enabled the county to hire a covered-bridge craftsman–Arnold Graton–to re-create the bridge using salvageable pieces of the original.

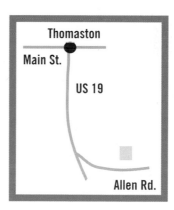

Big Chief Mill

11 | *Big Chief Mill*

Powered by: Overshot wheel
Water body: Lanahassee Creek
755 Mill Pond Road, Buena Vista 31803
N32 14 06 W84 33 35.9
Tourism Region: Presidential Pathways

DRIVING DIRECTIONS

From the intersection of GA 26 and GA 41 in Buena Vista, go south on GA 41 for 0.7 mile. Turn right on Pineville Road and go 4.0 miles. Turn left on Mill Pond Road and proceed 1.8 miles. The mill is on the left.

HISTORY

The Big Chief Mill was built in 1994 on the site of an earlier mill. The millstones came from a mill in nearby Webster County, which was operated by the uncle of B.E. Powell, the current owner of Big Chief. The mill is operational and produces Big Chief Corn Meal.

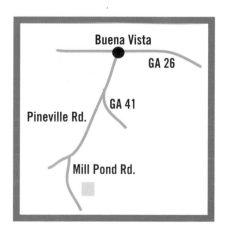

Overshot wheel powered by Powell's Millpond

Boyd Mill

The millstone encasement within the mill

Historic sign for Hearon's
Mill, Preston, Georgia

The miller's house and boathouse on the millpond

12 Boyd Mill aka Hearon's Mill aka Davenport's Mill

Powered by: Turbine

Water body: Long Branch Creek

580 Millpond Road, Preston 31824

N31 58 07.5 W84 32 39.8

Tourism Region: Presidential Pathways

Boyd Mill

DRIVING DIRECTIONS

From Preston, go south on GA 41 or Washington Street for 4.3 miles. Turn left (east) on Centerpoint Road and travel 2.7 miles. Turn right on Macedonia Church Road and go 1.2 miles. Take the second right onto Millpond Road. The mill is 0.6 mile on the right.

HISTORY

Built by John Boyd circa 1870, the mill went through several owners until William Davenport acquired the property in 1932. To provide electricity, Davenport added a generator, which was rare in rural 1930s Georgia. He also built a sawmill on the property. The dam broke in the 1940s, destroying the generator. The sawmill was demolished in 1969. The mill was idle until Henry S. Hearon Jr. purchased the mill and surrounding property in 1946. Hearon grew corn on the family farm and ground it into meal for delivery to stores in the surrounding counties. He operated the mill until 1963. His son, who used the miller's house as a second residence, purchased the property and mill in 1983. The mill was placed on the National Register of Historic Places in 2009.

The mill is at the edge of a pond created by a 400-foot-long earthen dam. The hydropower was controlled by a sluice gate, which sent water through a penstock to acti-

vate the mill turbine. Corn was carried via a canvas conveyor to the second floor, where it was sifted and cleaned before dropping to the 48-inch grinding stones on the first floor. The stones and some of the equipment are still in the mill.

In addition to the mill, today there is a miller's house, a boathouse, and assorted outbuildings on the property—all used as a second residence. You can see the mill and millpond from the road, but all are on private property.

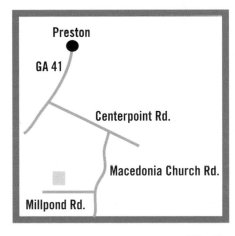

13 *Coheelee Creek Covered Bridge*

Construction type: Modified Queen Post
Water body: Coheelee Creek
GA 62 & Old River Road, Blakely 39823
N31 18 23.1 W85 04 43.4
Tourism Region: Plantation Trace

Coheelee Creek Covered Bridge

DRIVING DIRECTIONS

From Blakely, drive west on GA 62/Columbia Road for 10.2 miles. Turn right on Old River Road and go 1.6 miles. Stay right on Old River Road. When you see the sign for Coheelee Creek Park, continue straight. The bridge is 200 feet ahead on the left.

HISTORY

This is the southernmost original covered bridge in the United States. The 96-foot bridge was built in 1891 at the old McDonald Ford on Coheelee Creek. The bridge uses steel rods as tension members in the truss design. The angled rods make it unique in Georgia. The bridge fell into disuse. In 1984, concerned citizens embarked on a restoration. Today, the bridge makes a scenic setting as it spans Coheelee Creek with a small waterfall downstream. The bridge is not open to traffic, but Fannie Askew Williams Park, located next to the bridge, offers picnicking facilities. The area is a rare setting because there are not many waterfalls in southwest Georgia, but it makes a beautiful setting in the Wiregrass region near the Chattahoochee River's Alabama/Georgia boundary line. Across GA 80, south of the park, Coheelee Creek Public Use Area offers 16-29 free campsites.

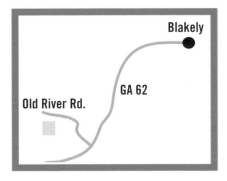

Sparta Mill

PART IV

The Southeast

The Southeast region is similar to The Southwest. The northern area extends into the Blue Ridge or north Georgia mountains. Because of the relatively flat topography of the southern portion of Georgia, there are few gristmills left in the coastal plain area. Historically, mills that were built required a millpond. The Southeast contains nineteen gristmills and six covered bridges.

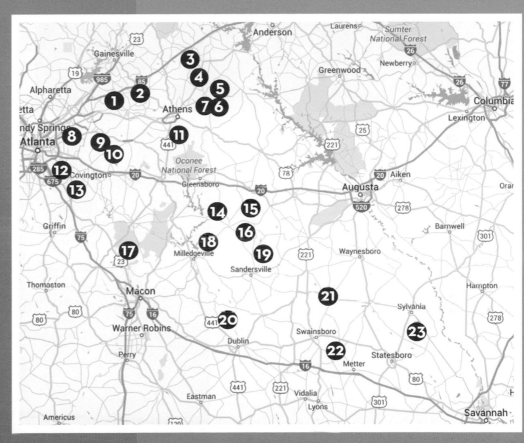

The milldam, located about 50 yards upstream from the mill

Note how the mill was raised approximately five feet to protect the building from floods.

1 *Swann's Mill aka Freeman's Mill aka Alcovy River Grist Mill*

Powered by: Overshot wheel

Water body: Alcovy River

1401 Alcovy Road, Lawrenceville 30045

770-904-3500

www.gwinnettcounty.com

N33 57 44.7 W83 55 36.4

Tourism Region: Atlanta Metro

Swann's Mill

DRIVING DIRECTIONS

From the intersection of GA 20 and US 29 in Lawrenceville, go east on US 29 for 2.1 miles to Sweet Gum Road. Turn right and proceed 1.0 mile. Turn left onto Alcovy Road and continue straight to a four-way stop. Continue straight through the stop. The entrance is on the left.

HISTORY

John Griffin Loveless and Levi J. Loveless originally constructed this mill between 1868-79. An 1880 census record shows the mill ran ten hours a day, year-round, producing 40 barrels of wheat flour, 14,400 pounds of cornmeal, and 54,000 pounds of feed per year.

Ownership has changed several times. Following the Loveless brothers, W. Scott Freeman and his son ran the mill. It changed hands again in 1915. In 1946, Lewis Swann purchased the property. The mill stayed in operation until the late twentieth century. In 2002, Gwinnett County acquired the property and converted it into a park.

A view of the milldam, looking upstream from the mill. Water is delivered to the overshot wheel via a pipe.

2 Sell's Mill

Powered by: Overshot wheel

Water body: Indian Creek

8783 Jackson Trail Road, Hoschton 30558

706-367-6350

www.jacksoncountygov.com

Hours: 8 AM-6 PM daily

N34 05 04.3 W83 43 46.2

Tourism Region: Northeast Georgia Mountains

Sell's Mill

DRIVING DIRECTIONS

From I-85, take Exit 129 for GA 53 East. Follow GA 53 East through Hoschton for 2.9 miles. Turn left on Jackson Trail Road. Sell's Mill Park is on the right after 1.0 mile.

HISTORY

The mill, which opened in 1914, was built to supply electricity as well as to grind grains for bread. Frank Sell, a legislator from Jackson County, owned the mill. Corn was ground there as late as the 1990s. In 2005, Jackson County purchased and renovated the mill for use as a park. Today, visitors can enjoy the shoals, waterwheel, mill building, and several nice hiking trails.

On the way to the mill, you pass through Braselton. At the intersection of GA 53 and Frances Street is the abandoned Enterprise Flour and Grist Mill. Built around 1900, it was a major milling operation with a daily capacity of producing 50-70 barrels of flour and 300 bushels of meal. It probably stopped operation in the 1950s. The mill building still retains most of the equipment, all of which is in remarkably good condition. The building has been renovated and is open for tours.

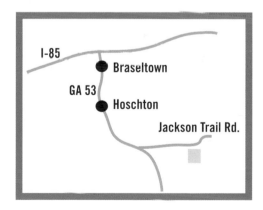

Cromer's Mill Covered Bridge

3 Cromer's Mill Covered Bridge

Construction type: Town's Lattice Truss
Water body: Nails Creek
20 Cromer's Bridge Road, Royston 30662
N34 16 30.3 W83 15 57.3
Tourism Region: Northeast Georgia Mountains

DRIVING DIRECTIONS

Northbound on I-85, take Exit 57 to GA 51. Go 5.3 miles to GA 106. Turn right and go south for 1.7 miles. The bridge is to the left of the bridge that crosses Nails Creek. Immediately after crossing the creek, turn left onto Baker Road. Park off the highway, where there is a parking area.

HISTORY

The Cromers settled on Nails Creek in 1845. The family operated a woolen mill near this site. Subsequently there was a cotton gin, flourmill, and sawmill in this area, though all the operations ceased by 1943. In 1907, the county contracted with James M. "Pink" Hunt to build the present 110-foot bridge. The bridge is open to foot traffic.

Cromer's Mill Covered Bridge

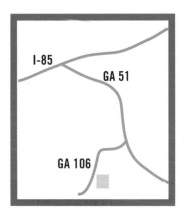

Mason's Mill

4 Mason's Mill

Powered by: Turbine

Water body: Masons Mill Creek

4909 General Daniels Avenue North,
   Danielsville 30633

N34 11 20.1 W83 12 14.1

Tourism Region: Northeast Georgia Mountains

Mason's Mill

DRIVING DIRECTIONS

At the intersection of GA 98 and US 29 in Danielsville, go north on US 29 for 4.5 miles. The mill is on the left, just before crossing Masons Mill Creek.

HISTORY

There is little available information regarding Mason's Mill. Although, it is not known when the mill was built, the Phillips family now owns it. Local people recall that it was the focal point of community social events and the millpond was a popular location for picnics and swimming. The dam collapsed some years ago. The mill is in poor condition and unsafe to enter. It is on private land but is easily visible from the road.

A view upstream of the milldam. The owner reports he hopes to restore the dam.

Remains of mill gears found on mill property

5 Osley Mill

Powered by: Overshot wheel
Water body: Holly Creek
1082 Osley Mill Road, Comer 30629
N34 05 24 W83 03 01
Tourism Region: Northeast Georgia Mountains

Osley Mill

DRIVING DIRECTIONS

From Comer, go 7.3 miles on GA 72 East. Turn left on Paoli Road and go 2.3 miles. Make a slight right onto Osley Mill Road, which is a dirt road. The mill is on the right after 1.2 miles.

HISTORY

According to an interview with the current owner, the mill was built circa 1790. The water was delivered via an underground pipe to an overshot wheel from a dam about 0.2 mile upstream. It is now a private residence. At first glance the structure is not recognizable as a mill. Machinery and old millstones are scattered around the grounds. The owner reports that the wheel from the mill is now used as a small Ferris wheel at the Comer County fairgrounds.

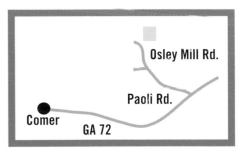

6 *Watson Mill Bridge*

Construction type: Town's Lattice Truss

Water body: South Fork of the Broad River

650 Watson Mill Road, Comer 30629

706-783-5349

www.gastateparks.org

Hours: 7AM-10 PM; December 1-February 28, office and campground are closed.

N34 01 37.1 W83 04 29.2

Tourism Region: Classic South

Watson Mill Bridge

DRIVING DIRECTIONS

From Comer, go south on GA 22 W for 1.8 miles. Turn left onto Watson Mill Road. Go 3.0 miles to Watson Mill State Park. The bridge is immediately visible upon entry. Normal state park entrance fees apply.

HISTORY

This bridge, along with the park, is considered one of the more picturesque state parks. The 229 feet across the South Fork of the Broad River make this the longest covered bridge in the state. The son of Horace King, Washington (W. W.) King, built the bridge in 1885. Horace King was a freed slave and a famous covered bridge builder. You can read more about Horace King's interesting life in the Red Oak Creek Covered Bridge entry in the Southwest section. This structure replaced an earlier structure the original owner, Gabriel Watson, had built.

At the start of the twentieth century, Jefferson Mills in Crawfordville purchased the mill south of the bridge and built a hydroelectric dam. Power was produced until the 1950s, but little remains of the mill today. In 1971, the state began restoration, opening the state park in 1973. The park has a nice campground and excellent horse trails. In the summer, the shoals below the bridge are a popular location to cool off.

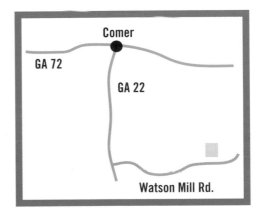

Howard's Covered Bridge

7 Howard's Covered Bridge

Construction type: Town's Lattice Truss

Water body: Big Clouds Creek

420 Chandler Silver Road, Comer 30629

N33 59 09.6 W83 08 00.9

Tourism Region: Classic South

Howard's Covered Bridge

DRIVING DIRECTIONS

From Athens, take GA 72 east to Colbert. Turn right (south) on Fourth Street, then left on Eighth Avenue (Smithonia-Colbert Road). After about 1.9 miles, this becomes Smithonia Road. After 3.8 more miles, turn left on Chandler Silver Road/Wildwood Lane. The bridge is on the right after 0.1 mile.

HISTORY

Historical records show a "Mr. Hunt" was the original builder. This was probably the same James M. "Pink" Hunt who supposedly built Cromer's Mill Bridge. The current bridge, which was built as a replacement in 1904-5, was named after a pioneer family who settled near Big Clouds Creek in the 1700s. At 164 feet, with a main span of 130 feet, the bridge once had the longest main span of any surviving bridges. At some point, a wooden pier was built to shore up the long span, so Howard's Bridge can no longer make that claim.

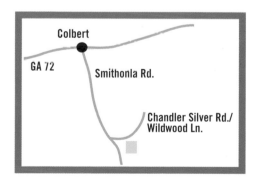

Stone Mountain Bridge

Stone Mountain Mill

Interior of the bridge

8 Stone Mountain Mill and Bridge

Mill powered by: Overshot wheel

Bridge construction type: Town's Lattice Truss

Water body: Stone Mountain Lake

1000 Robert E. Lee Boulevard, Stone Mountain 30083

800-401-2407

www.stonemountainpark.com

Hours: see website

N33 48 56.7 W84 08 47.5

Tourism Region: Atlanta Metro

Stone Mountain Mill and Bridge

DRIVING DIRECTIONS

Traveling on I-285 on the east side of Atlanta, take Exit 39B to US 78 East. Travel 7.7 miles on US 78 to Exit 8 and follow exit ramp to the east gate entrance of Stone Mountain Park.

HISTORY

The directions will take you to the entrance to Stone Mountain Park, which requires a parking fee. At the entrance, you receive a map of the park that gives detailed directions to the gristmill and covered bridge.

Washington W. King built the 151-foot-long covered bridge in 1891. At that time, it spanned the Oconee River in Clarke County. The bridge was sold for one dollar and moved to its present site at Stone Mountain in 1965.

The gristmill, originally built in 1869, was moved to the park from its original location near Ellijay, Georgia.

Rockdale County Covered Bridge

9 Rockdale County Covered Bridge aka Haralson Mill Covered Bridge

Construction type: Decorative Town's Lattice Truss

Water body: Mill Rock Creek

4501 Haralson Mill Road NE, Conyers 30013

N33 45 42.6 W83 57 26.8

Tourism Region: Historic Heartland

Rockdale County Covered Bridge

DRIVING DIRECTIONS

From I-20, take Exit 82 for GA 20/138. GA 138 splits and goes east. Stay on GA 20 for 8.3 miles. Turn right on Bethel Road NE. Go 0.7 mile and turn left on Haralson Mill Road NE. Go 1.7 miles to the bridge. It is adjacent to Randy Poynter Lake at Black Shoals Park and Jack Turner Dam. There is a small parking area with a trail leading to the water's edge.

HISTORY

Although this is not a historical bridge because it was built in 1997, it is a beautiful bridge and worth a visit. Originally planned as a pre-stressed concrete bridge, the county planners decided to make it a landmark and designed a wooden superstructure with decorative lattice.

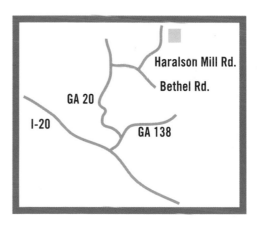

Dial Mill

All that remains of the overshot wheel

*An abandoned tractor at
the overgrown mill site*

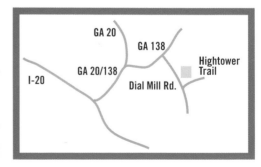

10 Dial Mill

Powered by: Overshot wheel

Water body: Little Haynes Creek

1200 Dial Mill Road, Conyers 30013

N33 42 40.2 W83 54 51.8

Tourism Region: Historic Heartland

Remains of a sign promoting a 1920 festival

DRIVING DIRECTIONS

From I-20, take Exit 82 for GA 20/138 and continue east on GA 138 for 6.8 miles. Turn right on Dial Mill Road. Go 0.9 mile to the intersection with Hightower Trail. The mill is on the left.

HISTORY

Located in what is now Rockdale County, the land was originally inhabited by the Creeks and Cherokees. The boundary between these two native nations was roughly the same as present-day Hightower Trail. Early white settlements grew up along the numerous waterways in the area. A series of treaties with the Creek Indians ceded the land south of the Hightower Trail to Georgia. When George Gilmer became governor in 1829, the state legislature passed laws forcing the Cherokee Nation to cede their lands north of the Hightower Trail. In 1830, Governor Gilmer granted to his friend Captain Allen Summers, of the Georgia Army, the land where the mill now stands. Officially, construction on the mill began in 1830 and was completed in 1833. There is strong reason to believe the mill was started in 1825 and near completion before 1830, when the grant was received. The mill used mortised joints, fitted and pegged perfectly. The main upright corners and 16-inch-square, hand-hewed beams in the middle extend all the way from the foundation to the third-floor roof. When Allen Summers died in 1854, his wife and son J. M. kept the property and allowed

Bill Puckett to continue to run the mill until he left in 1861 to enlist in the Georgia Volunteer Infantry. Johnny Wells ran the mill through the Civil War. In November 1864, General Sherman's army followed the Hightower Trail, stripping the land of food and destroying homes and means of production. Sherman's army was about to set fire to the mill when Puckett's wife, Winnie, personally pleaded with Sherman to spare the mill. Impressed by her boldness, he allowed the mill to stand. After the war, Bill Puckett returned to the mill and worked there until his death in 1894. The mill was used until the early to mid-1900s. It was added to the National Register of Historic Place in 1978. In 2003, the dam, flume, and overshot wheel were restored. Today, the grounds are overgrown, and it is difficult to see the mill when the trees have leaves. The flume is gone and the wooden wheel has almost rotted away, but the building itself is very solid. Surrounding the mill are several buildings and vehicles.

The mill is owned by Jim and Martina Gibboney. Recently Elizabeth Jones spearheaded a non-profit "Friends of Dial Mill" to raise funds for restoration of the mill and establish a small park on the surrounding land. More information on the mill and the foundation can be found at: www.dialmill.org or by calling Elizabeth Jones at 706-621-3580.

Elder's covered bridge

Buckets on a canvas belt were used to elevate corn to the second story of the mill.

Antique equipment in the interior of the mill

11 Elder's Mill and Covered Bridge

Mill powered by: Overshot wheel

Bridge construction type: Town's Lattice Truss

Water body: Rose Creek

Approximate Address: 144 Elder Mill Road, Watkinsville 30677

N 33 48 10.7 W83 21 49.6

Tourism Region: Historic Heartland

Elder's Mill

DRIVING DIRECTIONS

From Watkinsville, go south on GA 15 for 4.5 miles. Turn right onto Elder Mill Road. The bridge is 0.8 mile ahead. The mill is on the left, just before crossing the creek.

HISTORY

Nathaniel Richardson built the bridge in 1897. The 99-foot bridge originally crossed Calls Creek on the Athens-Watkinsville Road. In 1924, it was moved to its present site spanning Rose Creek. It is one of the few covered bridges in Georgia that continues to carry traffic without underlying steel beams. Nearby is Elder's Mill, which was built around the turn of the twentieth century. It was run by four generations of the Elder family. The mill ceased operations in 1941. Recently, there have been efforts to reopen the mill for tours.

Above: *A view of Main Street in Rex, Georgia, with the mill in background*

A sign on the side of Rex Mill

12 *Rex Mill*

Powered by: Overshot wheel
Water body: Big Cotton Indian Creek
3735 Mill Walk, Rex 30273
N 33 35 35.7 W 84 16 07.1
Tourism Region: Atlanta Metro

Rex Mill

DRIVING DIRECTIONS

Heading south on I-675, take Exit 2 onto US 23/GA 42 West. After 0.1 mile, turn right onto Evan's Drive. Travel for 1.0 mile and turn right on Rex Road. Go about 0.5 mile. Turn left onto Colonnade Dr. After traveling about 150 feet, make a right turn on Mill Walk. The mill is on the left as you cross the creek.

HISTORY

The mill sits along the Big Cotton Indian Creek in the small village of Rex, only 20 miles from central Atlanta. Built circa 1830, it was still in use in the 1930s and 1940s when surrounding farmers brought grain in for milling. When I. L. Hollingsworth built the mill, he named it after his dog Rex. In the vicinity, there is an old steel bridge and a quaint village. Michelle Obama's great-great-great grandmother was a slave on a nearby plantation. Several movies have been filmed in the area.

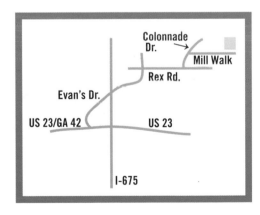

Milldam and raceway

Ruins left after a fire in 2000

13 Miller's Mill aka McDonough Mill

Powered by: Overshot wheel

Water body: Big Cotton Indian Creek

3099 GA 155 North, McDonough 30281

N 33 32 02 W84 08 20.3

Tourism Region: Atlanta Metro

The only building standing after the fire in 2000.

DRIVING DIRECTIONS

At the intersection of GA 20 (John Frank Ward Boulevard) and GA 155 in McDonough, go north on GA 155 for 6.2 miles. The mill is on the left after crossing Big Cotton Indian Creek.

HISTORY

The original mill was built circa 1850 by Silas Moseley across the creek from the present site. It had a small overshot wheel. The original dam was a log dam. About 1917-18, the present dam was built. In 1925, D. S. Miller bought the property. At the time, there was a cotton gin. Miller added an overshot wheel to run the gristmill and another overshot wheel to run the cotton gin. Herman Miller is the present owner. His grandmother's cousin bought and built the two-story building on the present site. Herman's grandfather added a turbine to run the planing mill. In 1962, a flood destroyed the race to the gristmill. In the late 1980s, the raceway was rebuilt. The gristmill was restored and made operational. In April 2000, a homeless person lit a fire in the building for warmth, and the gristmill burned down.

Although you can see the entire complex from the road, stop at the old country store on the highway, operated by Herman Miller, and enjoy his stories.

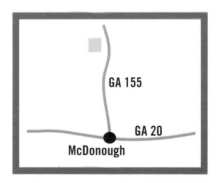

Sparta Mill

The drive pulley and shaft

Millstones

The separator

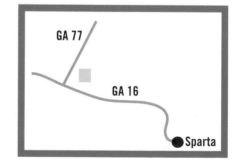

14 Sparta Mill aka Millmore Mill aka Harris Mill aka Baxter's Mill
(locally also known as "The Mill at Shoulderbone")

Powered by: Turbine

Water body: Shoulderborne Creek

Intersection of GA 16 and GA 77, Sparta 31087

N33 20 20 W83 04 44.4

Tourism Region: Classic South

Heavy scales for weighing grain loads

DRIVING DIRECTIONS:

Leave Sparta on GA 16 W and go 7.8 miles to the intersection with GA 77. The mill is on the right.

HISTORY

This mill was built circa 1790. On the shores of the creek near the site of today's mill, the Treaty of Shoulderbone Creek was signed between the Creek Confederation and the state of Georgia in 1786. Probably the first mill builder was Revolutionary War soldier Major Andrew Baxter (1750-1814). From the early 1900s until the 1930s, the area was known as Harris Mill. The area, now known as Millmore, reached its peak in the 1930s and 40s under the direction of the Lovejoy family. At one time, it had 35 employees and ground all the cornmeal sold in Piggly Wiggly grocery stores throughout the state. When the demand for cornmeal and local farming began to diminish, the mill fell into disuse. Circa mid-1990s, Ellen Stewart purchased the mill and refurbished one of the three turbines. It operated briefly but has been idle in recent years. The interior of the mill was thoroughly cleaned in November 2014.

Ellen's daughter, Scarlett Sears, is the current owner. She recently repaired and improved the exterior appearance of the mill building and surrounding grounds. She is now in the process of re-purposing the mill operations–primarily hydropower–but she is keeping the ability to grind meal. She is completely refurbishing the three turbines that are in the lowest level of the mill and installing generators and associated equipment to generate electricity that will tie into the local coop power company—Washington EMC. Her plans include maintaining the appearance of the mill and keeping all the original equipment in place. Long-term plans are to occasionally open the mill to the public for tours and/or establish the facility and grounds as a special events venue. Nearby is the Shoulderbone Plantation, still on its original 2,000-acres, complete with barns and other outbuildings.

A view of the mill with turbine house and drive shaft to the right

The mill as viewed from across the Ogeechee River

One of the mill's two millstones

Inside the turbine house, looking down the long drive shaft to the mill. Note the wooden teeth on the primary bevel gear in the foreground.

15 Ogeechee River Mill

Powered by: Turbine
Water body: Ogeechee River
262 Reynolds Road, Warrenton 30828
704-465-2195 for tours
Email: ogeecheerivermill@yahoo.com
N33 21 51.6 W82 48 21
Tourism Region: Classic South

Ogeechee River Mill

DRIVING DIRECTIONS

Leaving Warrenton on US 278N, go 0.7 mile. Turn left on Mayfield Road (GA 165). Go 8.5 miles. Once you cross the river, the road becomes Warrenton Road. Go about 0.1 mile past the river. Turn right on Ogeechee Road. The mill is 0.1 mile down the road on the left. *Note:* The address is misleading. Do not turn onto Reynolds Road. Continue on Warrenton Road as outlined above.

HISTORY

This corn mill has been in operation since 1826. A map drawn in 1847 listed Latimer's Mill at Mayfield on the Warren County side of the river. In 1916-18, the property was sold to Arthur Reynolds Sr., who operated the property until the early 1930s. Between 1931 and 1933, Arthur Reynolds Jr. replaced the worn-out wooden dam with a new dam constructed of Hancock County granite. He moved the mill to the present site, where it is less prone to floods.

In 2005, Missy Garner, who currently owns the mill, moved her family cattle ranch operation from Florida. She found the new property came with the bonus of a working gristmill. In spring of 2015, Missy was working on improvements to the mill and is still operating the mill for local farmers and outlets. You can arrange mill tours by calling 706-465-2195.

Hamburg Mill

16 *Hamburg Mill*

Powered by: Turbine

Water body: Little Ogeechee River

6701 Hamburg State Park Road, Mitchell 30820

478-552-2393

www.gastateparks.org

**Hours: see website; park is open March 15
    through November 30.**

N33 12 20.8 W82 46 44.8

Tourism Region: Classic South

Hamburg Mill

DRIVING DIRECTIONS

From Sparta, drive on GA 16E for 12.1 miles. Turn right onto State Route 248. Go 6.6 miles into Hamburg State Park. The mill is on the right.

HISTORY

The Warthen family built the first mill in 1875 just 75 feet upstream from the present site. The original mill operated until the early 1900s. The mill changed hands several times before the Gilmore brothers finally acquired it. They built the present mill, dam, and cotton gin in 1921-22. The mill was set up to grind both flour and cornmeal. Eventually, the property was sold to Tarbutton and Rawlings, who deeded the property to the state in 1968. The state park, where the mill is located today, offers camping, fishing, and hiking. During special events or festivals at the park, the mill is open and used for grinding corn.

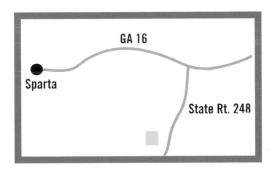

Juliette Mill

Downtown Juliette, Georgia, which was the setting for the movie Fried Green Tomatoes. *The Whistle Stop Café is on the right.*

17 *Juliette Mill*

Powered by: Turbine

Water body: Ocmulgee River

Approximate Address:

   443 McCrackin Street, Juliette 31046

478-992-8886

N33 06 16.7 W83 47 51

Tourism Region: Historic Heartland

DRIVING DIRECTIONS

From McDonough, go south on US 23. At the intersection with GA 83, continue south on US 23. After 3.6 miles, turn left on Juliette Road. Go 0.7 mile and turn right on McCrackin Street. After 300 feet, arrive at the Whistle Stop Café. The mill is visible straight ahead.

Juliette Mill

HISTORY

About 1845, the Leary brothers built the first of three mills on the west bank of the Ocmulgee River. In 1856, Joseph and Isaac Smith acquired the Leary gristmill and opened a sawmill and custom gristmill on the east bank. The operation survived the Civil War. In 1879, Dr. W. P. Glover assumed leadership of the gristmill and expanded operations on the east bank. In 1899, he took on additional partners and continued to expand operations, building a cotton mill on the east bank. In 1906, the partners replaced the 1845 Leary gristmill with what was considered the largest water-powered stone-grinding mill in the world. In 1927, the third and current mill was built to replace the gristmill, which had burned the year before. Market conditions eventually forced the gristmill to close in 1957. The cotton mill closed in 1965. The community

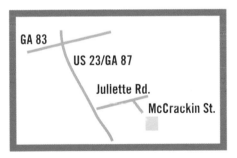

declined until Hollywood revived the village of Juliette as the fictional community of Whistle Stop for the movie, *Fried Green Tomatoes*. The Whistle Stop Café, featured in the movie, still serves customers. The mill, owned by Les White, is a private residence. In 2016, the mill was reportedly for sale.

O'Quinn's Mill

O'Quinn's pond

18 O'Quinn's Mill

Powered by: Turbine

Water body: Town Creek

243 Deepstep Road, Milledgeville 31061

N33 03 00 W83 06 04.3

Tourism Region: Historic Heartland

O'Quinn's Mill

DRIVING DIRECTIONS

At the junction of Jefferson Street and GA 22 in Milledgeville, go east on GA 22 for 4.1 miles. Make a slight right onto GA 24 Spur South. Go 3.3 miles. Turn left onto Deepstep Road NE. The mill is 1.4 miles on the left.

HISTORY

Colonel Thaddeus Holt built the first mill on this site in 1807. Colonel Holt was a prominent landowner in Baldwin County. He served in the Georgia Assembly in 1809 and was a lieutenant colonel in the War of 1812. He was killed in October 1813 by John "Whiskey" Jones, while travelling between his plantations.

Colonel Holt was the great-great grandfather of Doris Duke, who in 1924 inherited a fortune estimated as high as $1.3 billion dollars (in 2016 dollars) from her father, tobacco and hydroelectric tycoon James Buchanan Duke. In the 1930s, Doris was known as "the richest girl in the world."

The mill was rebuilt in 1832. In 2003, there were reportedly three runs of millstones. The mill produced and sold flour with plans to add a sawmill, a cane mill, and a shingle mill. In 2015, the mill appeared closed, with a considerable collection of equipment and debris around the area. The mill is easily seen from the road, but there is nowhere to park.

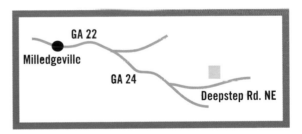

Downstream from the Jordan millpond

One of several old vehicles seen on the property

19 Jordan Mill

Powered by: Turbine

Water body: Kittrell Creek

Approximate address:

   1894 Jordan Mill Pond Road, Davisboro 31018

N33 02 10 W82 40 30

Tourism Region: Classic South

Jordan Mill

DRIVING DIRECTIONS

At the junction of Church Street and GA 15 in Sandersville, go north on GA 15 for 1.7 miles. Turn right on Fall Line Freeway (GA 88). Go 6.4 miles, then turn left on Jordan Mill Pond Road. The mill is 2.0 miles ahead on the left.

HISTORY

Joseph Henry Hines moved to Whitehall, a 4,000-acre plantation, in Washington County in 1857. The mill he operated at Whitehall became known as the Hines Mill. During the Civil War, Joseph Hines operated the mill continuously to provide grain to families and soldiers. Fortunately, a Union officer was convinced not to destroy the mill during Sherman's March to the Sea. The daughter of Joseph Hines married Stephen Gilmore Jordan in 1873. She eventually inherited the plantation and the mill and renamed it Jordan Mill. The original mill burned in the 1920s. The present mill, which was rebuilt in 1928, continued operations until circa 1955. Now the mill building is used for storage. The millpond is a popular location for fishing and picnicking.

Chappell's Mill complex—the mill is on the left, the office is in the center, and grain storage silos are on the right.

20 Chappell's Mill

Powered by: Turbine

Water body: South Sandy Creek

Chappells Pond Dam, Chappell Mill Rd., Dublin 31021

N32 39 42.6 W83 03 10.2

Tourism Region: Magnolia Midlands

Note: This mill should not be confused with Chappell's Mill in the Southwest section of this book.

Chappell's Mill

DRIVING DIRECTIONS

At the intersection of US 441 and US 80 in Dublin, go 12.4 miles north on US 441. Turn left on Chappell Mill Road (GA 421). Go 0.3 mile. The mill is on the right.

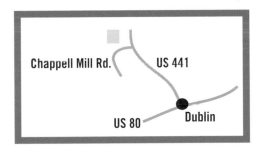

HISTORY

The exact date the mill was built is uncertain, but most likely John or Thomas Gilbert built it about 1811. Not long after, James Stanley II purchased the mill and the surrounding area. The mill was spared from Sherman's March to the Sea when Major James Duggan and an elderly slavewoman tricked the Union cavalry into believing a squad of Wheeler's cavalry was coming to secure the bridge and thus diverted them away from the mill.

Members of the Stanley family operated the mill until 1868, when the sons and sons-in-law of Ira Stanley purchased the mill. One of the buyers was son-in-law James W. Chappell. From that point on, it was known as Chappell's Mill. The mill operated on water power until about 1950, when it was converted to electric power. The mill provided cornmeal to grocery stores throughout the state. In 1997, government regulations required the installation of prohibitively expensive equipment, so the owners decided to close the mill after 186 years of continuous operation.

Today, extensive outbuildings and grain storage silos surround the mill, which sits beside a beautiful dam.

McKinney's Pond Mill

McKinney's Pond Restaurant

21 *McKinney's Pond Mill*

Powered by: Turbine

Water body: Mill Creek

181 McKinney Pond Road, Midville 30441

478-589-7186

www.mckinneyspond.net

N32 47 27.4 W82 13 09.9

Tourism Region: Classic South

McKinney's Pond Mill

DRIVING DIRECTIONS

At the intersection of GA 17 and GA 56 in Midville, go 2.5 miles south on GA 56. Turn left on Old Savannah Road. Go 1.3 miles to McKinney Pond Road and turn left. After 0.7 mile, McKinney's Pond Restaurant is on the left. The mill is a short walk straight ahead.

HISTORY

Today, the popular McKinney's Pond Restaurant, which opened in 1938, sits on the property near the mill. Although there is little recorded history about the mill, the long, low dam across the pond was in existence when the first white settlers came to Emanuel County. Some believe the Lower Muskogee Creeks built the dam more than 300 years ago, making it the oldest man-made structure in the county. The mill was powered by water from McKinney's Pond, a 200-acre spring-fed cypress pond. It was operational in 1990 but is now deteriorating.

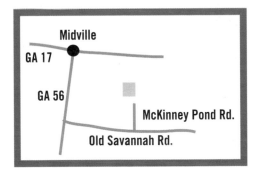

A view from downstream below the mill

Detail under the mill showing the horizontal shaft, which drove the different mill operations.

22 *Parrish Mill and Covered Bridge*

Bridge construction type: N/A

Mill powered by: Turbine

Water body: Watson Pond on Fifteen Mile Creek

George L. Smith State Park

371 George L. Smith State Park Road, Twin City 30471

478-763-2759

www.gastateparks.org

Hours: 7 AM-10 PM; there is a parking fee.

N32 32 40.1 W82 07 36.6

Tourism Region: Classic South

Parrish Mill and Covered Bridge

DRIVING DIRECTIONS

From I-16, take Exit 104 to GA 23 North. Go 13.6 miles north on GA 23. Turn right on George L. Smith State Park Road. It is 1.9 miles to the park entrance. The bridge is visible as you enter the park.

HISTORY

This structure is unique because it is both a covered bridge and a mill, all in one building. Constructed in 1880, the mill/bridge was built over a dam. The water going over the dam on Fifteen Mile Creek powered the mill. Doors on either end allowed traffic to pass through. The mill/bridge operated as a combination gristmill, sawmill, and cotton gin.

It is now located in George L. Smith State Park, which is popular for sightseeing, boating, kayaking, camping, and fishing. The Parrish Mill Pond, also known as Watson Pond, is dotted with beautiful cypress trees, which emit an acid turning the water black, but it does not affect the quality of the water.

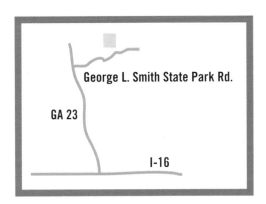

In May, lily pads on the millpond are in bloom. Note: At the lower right of building is the inlet gate for water that drives the turbine.

An interior view of a workbench in the mill

An interior shot of grinding stones. Corn is hand-fed into the hopper.

23 Robbins Grist Mill

Powered by: Turbine

Water body: Ogeechee Creek Grist Mill Pond

5564 Savannah Highway (GA 21), Sylvania 30467

912-857-3776

Hours: 9 AM-noon; first and third Saturday of the month between November and April.

N32 38 11.8 W81 33 36.7

Tourism Region: Magnolia Midlands

Robbins Grist Mill

DRIVING DIRECTIONS

From the central square of Sylvania, head south on South Main Street/GA 21 for 9.5 miles. Watch for the Robbins Grist Mill sign to turn right. The mill is approximately 0.25 mile down the road. The GPS coordinates are for the turn-off point at GA 21.

HISTORY

The mill was originally built in 1803, but General Sherman's troops destroyed the mill during the Civil War. After Sherman's troops left, William H. Robbins's grandmother gave the mill to a merchant in exchange for food. Later, William Robbins received a pharmacology degree from Mercer University. He was involved in assorted businesses in the 1930s and 40s, but always kept his eye on the mill and property. In 1937, he began making payments on the mill. He worked to restore the dam and the mill as he could. He completed the restoration and ground his first corn on September 4, 1954.

The mill operates two Saturdays a month and welcomes the public during that time. The owners are open to visitors at other times if you make prior arrangements by calling ahead at 912-857-3776.

Coheelee Creek Covered Bridge